Think Like an Interviewer

Think Like an Interviewer

Your Job Hunting Guide to Success

Ronald J. Auerbach

iUniverse, Inc.
New York Bloomington Shanghai

Think Like an Interviewer
Your Job Hunting Guide to Success

Copyright © 2008 by Ronald Auerbach

iUniverse books may be ordered through booksellers or by contacting:

iUniverse
1663 Liberty Drive
Bloomington, IN 47403
www.iuniverse.com
1-800-Authors (1-800-288-4677)

Because of the dynamic nature of the Internet, any Web addresses or links contained in this book may have changed since publication and may no longer be valid.

The information contained in this publication is provided solely for informational purposes. It was designed to provide accurate and authoritative information with regard to the topics covered. It is sold with the understanding that the publisher is not engaged in rendering any legal, accounting, or other professional advice. If legal advice or other expert assistance is required, the services of a qualified professional should be sought.

Library of Congress Control Number: 2008922074

ISBN: 978-0-595-45212-5 (pbk)
ISBN: 978-0-595-89521-2 (ebk)

Printed in the United States of America

Dedication

This book is dedicated to my family and friends. Your support, willingness to help, and advice were extremely helpful in making this book a success. I want you all to know that you have my ever-lasting and deepest gratitude.

Lastly, I would like to thank the countless strangers for offering me your comments and suggestions. When I asked for your opinions, you could easily have said no. But your kindness and willingness to help a total stranger is much appreciated. For that, I thank you.

Every single one of you have helped to make *Think Like an Interviewer* a success.

Dedication

This book is dedicated to my family and friends. Your support, willingness to help, and advice were extremely helpful in making this book a success. I want you all to know that you have my ever-lasting and deepest gratitude.

Lastly, I would like to thank the countless strangers for offering me your comments and suggestions. When I asked for your opinions, you could easily have said no. But your kindness and willingness to help a total stranger is much appreciated. For that, I thank you.

Every single one of you have helped to make *Think Like an Interviewer* a success.

About the Author

Ron Auerbach has worked in different jobs and industries. He's taught subjects ranging from accounting to web design and has conducted several workshops.

Having an M.B.A. and Human Resource training, he truly enjoys sharing his knowledge with others and helping them succeed. The people he's advised have been very appreciative.

Table of Contents

Introduction

What's your favorite joke? Believe it or not, the decision to hire you can all depend on the answer you give. How do I know? Because I was once hired for a position based upon my answer to this very question! Why would an interviewer ask it? How should you handle it? How could a job offer hinge on your response?

As you'll soon learn in the pages of *Think Like an Interviewer*, every interview question is being asked for a very specific reason. Interviewing success lies in your ability to correctly identify those reasons and molding your answers around them. Guessing right can lead to success, while guessing wrong may lead to failure. *Think Like an Interviewer* will help you guess right!

It will help you discover the real, and often hidden purpose(s) of many interview questions. Armed with this knowledge in advance, you'll be in a much better position to mold your answers around them. This can give you that all important edge over your competition!

But unlike many other resources, I don't give you specific answers to use. That's because you *must* sound like yourself or you won't come across as believable. Part of what an interviewer does is match the resume to the person being interviewed. In other words, he or she looks to see if the person on paper appears and sounds like the one speaking. If the interviewer begins to question this at any time during your interview, your chances of landing that job decrease.

So what I do in *Think Like an Interviewer* is present you with the main purpose(s) behind the questions. You'll get solid and practical advice designed to help improve your chances of hearing those beloved words, "You're hired!" Whether or not you choose to follow my advice is totally up to you. But I firmly believe your chances will be better with my help. Tipping the odds in your favor, even just a little bit, could mean the difference between success and failure.

Yet *Think Like an Interviewer* is much more than a book on successful interviewing. It's actually a full-blown job search book that covers: job applications, cover letters, resumes, and even a letter of resignation. So within these pages, you'll be gaining all the knowledge you need in order to improve your job hunting. And in today's tough job market, every little bit helps!

How tough is it today? Well *CBS News* reported on April 7, 2008 that job losses now average a whopping 77,000 per month! They also mentioned that temp jobs were down by 42,000. And the *U.S. Department of Labor's* April 4, 2008 report showed another 80,000 jobs were lost during March. That's the biggest loss in five years!

Manufacturing and construction jobs continued their decline. Yet healthcare, food services, and mining added jobs. In addition, the number of out-of-work Americans rose by 434,000 to just under 8 million! And the overall unemployment rate increased to 5.1%; the highest it's been in three years. It literally rose across the board: Adult men and women, Whites, African-Americans, and Hispanics.

The one exception was for teenagers, where the rate declined to 15.8 So anyone looking for work today knows exactly how tough it really is. And that's exactly why you need *Think Like an Interviewer*.

Oh by the way, in their May 2, 2008 report, the March job loss figure was revised upwards to 81,000. How many jobs did we loose during April? Well analysts were expecting a loss of 75,000, but we ended-up loosing just 20,000; something that may provide comfort to job seekers. But then again, April was the fourth straight month of job losses and brings the total loss of jobs for this year to 260,000. And the number of unemployed rose to a staggering 7.6 million! That's almost 1 million more than a year ago.

In addition, *NBC News* had a story on May 25, 2008 talking about the tough job market college students are facing. One student featured in the story thought her job search was over when she landed a paid internship. But unfortunately, the company recinded her job offer due to a hiring freeze. So the job market continues to be a tough one for anyone looking for work or worried about loosing their job.

Why should you feel confident in the information I'll be presenting? Well that's a very fair question and let me answer it by saying this. As an educator, I truly enjoy sharing my knowledge and expertise with others. It's the pure joy of seeing the faces light-up and in hearing the success stories that continues to motivate me. I will derive this same amount of pleasure from hearing about your happiness and success.

My experience includes having worked in a variety of fields. I've worked in different cities and states in jobs with varying levels of responsibilities. Now I teach and train others. So you'll be receiving advice from somebody who's "been there and done that." I also have the ability to simplify thing because of my academic and training background. This means everything will be presented in a way that's easily understood.

My ultimate goal with *Think like an Interviewer* is to improve your odds and tip the scale more to your side. But please realize and understand that there are no guarantees in life. So I won't guarantee that you'll get the job you want. However, in all my years of advising and helping people with their cover letters, resumes, and interviewing, I've noticed one thing. Those who have followed my advice seem to have done pretty well in their careers and are very appreciative of my help

Interviewing can be extremely subjective and complex. The questions a particular candidate might be asked can and do vary widely. Your best friend in helping you prepare for interviews is somebody who:

1. Keeps current with job market conditions
2. Works with others to improve their job hunting skills
3. Gives you the knowledge to succeed
4. Makes an honest assessment and offers practical advice
5. Is a skilled trainer who can motivate you

These are what I offer you in the pages of *Think Like an Interviewer*. But don't forget that you'll also get the information you need to make it to the interviewing stage. Remember, you dont simply walk into an interview in most cases. It'll usually come after you've submitted your cover letter and resume. So to even make it to the interview, you have to get past some hurdles. And that's exactly why I've included them too.

This is what makes *Think Like an Interviewer* the ideal resorce for any job hunter. And I'm pretty confident that you'll improve your chances by reading and following my advice. I want to wish you good luck in advance, hope you enjoy my book, and look forward to hearing about your successes!

PART 1:

Job search Overview

These chapters discuss the job hunting process and explain the various steps we go through. You'll learn:

1. The purpose of a cover letter, resume, and interview
2. Cover letter and resume formats
3. What information to include in a cover letter and resume

I urge you not to skip over these chapters because there's plenty of valuable information and good advice that can help improve your success. Besides, you have to get past these in order to make it to an interview!

The Hiring Process

Before we start talking about how to handle specific interview questions, let's outline the process of gaining employment. Job hunting is just like sales. You are selling yourself to a prospective employer in the hopes of getting an interview and being hired. So you need to approach the process from a sales perspective.

The job search process has five main steps:

1. You see a job advertised or make an inquiry
2. You submit a cover letter and/or resume
3. You interview, perhaps several times
4. You receive a job offer to consider
5. You accept the job and begin working

Now the most important part is the interview! Why? Because you can have the world's best cover letter and resume, but it'll be the interview that gets you the job. The reason is because:

→ A *cover letter's* purpose is to introduce yourself to a prospective employer. It briefly describes your background and why you're right for the job and/or field. It's to convince the employer to look at your resume for more details.

→ A *resume's* purpose is to provide details regarding your background. It expands on your cover letter and showcases your education, work experience, and skills.

→ An *interview's* purpose is to see whether you are the person you appear to be on paper. Up to this point, you've been nothing more than a piece of paper. An interview is the first time an employer can see and speak with you. This helps determine if you know your stuff and are the right one for the job. That's why doing extremely well in an interview is so critical to success! It's also why it's the main focus of this book.

The Cover Letter

Your cover letter should be short, sweet, and to the point. It should also be tailored to the job you want. *Appendix A* gives you a sample cover letter. Now here are some general tips to writing a successful cover letter:

1. Your main purpose is to briefly introduce yourself and direct attention to your resume for more details about your qualifications. An effective cover letter leave the reader wanting to know more. In other words, it peaks the reader's interest and gets him or her to look at your resume for more information.
2. Your letter should fill no more than 3/4 to one page. It should also not exceed four or five paragraphs in length. That's because you're giving a quick overview and not tons of details. Employers are busy and don't have lots of time to sift through lengthy inquiries. You want to impress the employer just enough to look at your resume and learn more.
3. Mold it to the job, profession, and company. Doing some research will definitely help accomplish this. This means possibly changing the wording or information contained in the letter. Many applicants will use a generic cover letter for all jobs. That's not a good idea! It should be tailored to the individual job and company.

Tip #1: Looking at the job description, and knowing something about what a person in that position might do, can help you tailor the letter.

For example, if the ad lists some responsibilities, then your letter can focus on your ability to handle them. This shows that you actually read the information and spent time revising your letter around it. You'll standout much better by doing this!

The Greeting

Your cover letter begins with the *salutation*, which is the greeting. Common ones are:

- ➜ Dear Sir or Madam
- ➜ To Whom It May Concern
- ➜ Dear Hiring Manager
- ➜ Dear Hiring Authority

Here is where you can make your first mistake! Some people will put a comma after their salutation; others will put a colon. Which one should it be? Does it matter? Yes, it does matter! When writing a personal letter, you would use a comma. But a cover letter is a business letter, which means you'd use a *colon*.

So the proper formatting would be:

➔ Dear Sir or Madam:
➔ To Whom It May Concern:
➔ Dear Hiring Manager:
➔ Dear Hiring Authority:

Some people don't feel addressing a letter to *Hiring Manager* or *Hiring Authority* is the most professional greeting. That's because sending your cover letter to someone who can do the hiring is a given. On the opposite side of the fence, some feel *Dear Sir or Madam* or *To Whom It May Concern* are outdated, too formal, or more impersonal.

There's even a letter format that some use today called *simplified style*. With this format, there's no greeting at all! Instead, you substitute a subject line that's in all caps (capital letters). This tells the reader in a nutshell what your letter is all about. And it's a popular way to write business correspondence today. However, some believe a greeting should be part of any letter.

The choice of how to address your letter is totally up to you. I'm simply giving you both sides so you can decide for yourself which greeting you feel would be best. If you're unsure, then you could always try different ones to see which gets the better response. But I don't really think it's going to make a huge difference! Job seekers have been using all these greetings for years with positive results. So it's more of a personal feeling towards one or the other.

Tip #2:   If possible, address your letter to a specific person

You'll look much better if you address your letter to a specific person rather than using one of the generic greetings from above. This makes your cover letter more personalized so you'll standout more. How can you find out who you should address your letter to? Easy, call the employer and ask! This way, you're taking initiative and spotlighting your researching abilities. And you'd be more than a piece of paper. You'd be a voice on the phone who sounds confident, professional, and knowledgeable!

That's if you know who the employer is. There may be times when you don't know who the employer is. The ad may only say to fax your resume to a certain phone number. Or you might not know who the person is because it's an e-mail address like rj@abccompany.com. All you have here are initials, but not the person's name.

Tip #3:   Many will simply fax their resume with one of the generic greeting. Or send an e-mail with the greeting *Dear RJ*. But here's something you could do to make yourself standout more and get noticed. Use a website like *www.theultimates.com* to find the name or phone number.

This site has white pages to find people, yellow pages to find companies, and an e-mail directory. They include *Yahoo*, *Dogpile*, *Worldpages*, and others.

- ➜ If you click on *yellow pages*, you'll be able to search by company name, address, or phone
- ➜ By clicking on *e-mail*, you can enter an e-mail address and get a name and company
- ➜ Clicking on *white* gives you the option to search for people by name

I've used the site many times and feel it's one of the best out there on the net. What's nice about it is you have several directories all in one spot. So you don't have to bounce around if one doesn't work. In addition, it opens the search results in a new window.

You can even search for companies by category. If you enter a search term into the *category* field, it'll bring up a list of companies in that area. You'll get their names, addresses, phone numbers, and a link for maps and driving directions. This can help you target specific types of companies or industries. It's also helpful if you're seeking work in another city or state.

If you're able to track down the employer, give them a call. Mention you'd like to apply for a particular job or are seeking employment. And then ask who you should address your cover letter to. Going this extra mile showcases your initiative and researching capabilities! You might even be transferred to someone who will do a phone interview right then and there. Or setup an interview.

But before you pick up the phone and call, I strongly suggest reading through the section on interviewing. That's because you only get one chance to make a good impression. So you must behave and handle it well.

Writing Your Cover Letter

Your first paragraph is very short—one or two sentences—and should:

- ➜ State the reason why you're writing. Is it in response to an ad? Is it to inquire if there are jobs available?

Tip #4: Yes, you can write a cover letter telling an employer you're looking for work. We call this a *blind cover letter* and it can be highly effective! This type of cover letter tells an employer you're looking for work and want to know if they have anything available for someone with your background. Initiative is a positive trait that will impress an employer. Your having the guts to contact me separates you from the others who simply wait for an ad to appear.

- ➜ When responding to a print ad or posting on the internet, I suggest you mention three things: The job, where you found it, and the ad or posting date.

Tip #5: Many applicants will only put the job name. But employers sometimes advertise the same position in multiple places and/or sections. They may even run different versions of the ad. Mentioning where you saw the ad or posting helps the employer measure the effectiveness of their advertising. This can help you standout from your competition.

For example, *I am responding to your April 18, 2007 ad in the Seattle Times for a Payroll Assistant.* Or *I am writing in response to your August 4, 2007 posting on CareerBuilder.com for a Machinist.*

➜ Say you're enclosing your resume for "consideration" or "review." For example, *I am responding to your April 18, 2007 ad in the Seattle Times for a Payroll Assistant, and have enclosed my resume for your consideration.* Or *I am writing in response to your August 4, 2007 posting on CareerBuilder.com for a Machinist. Attached is my resume for your review.*

Tip #6: A common mistake is to say you are enclosing a resume with an e-mail. *Enclosing* means physically mailing; *attaching* means e-mailing. It's sometimes these little things that get noticed.

The next paragraph or two should:

➜ *Briefly* highlight or summarize your background, education, and experience. It's a quick sales pitch to let me know what you're capable of, and why I should even look at your resume. In other words, it offers some details but not a whole lot. Just enough to say, "Interesting, tell me more!" The resume's purpose is to provide lots of details.

➜ Focus on what's relevant to the job, profession, and company. Mold it to the needs of the job and/or field. In other words, pick and choose the things that are most relevant to this job and profession.

Paragraph three or four should:

➜ State your willingness and availability to interview.

➜ Mention how you can be reached or contacted.

Tip #7: If an employer is unable to reach you on the first or second try, many will simply move on to the next person. That's why it's best to list all the ways an employer can reach you. Besides, you never know when and how an employer will try to contact you.

Your last paragraph should:

➜ Thank the employer for taking his or her time to consider your application. This is extremely important!

Tip #8: Include a brief restatement of why you're right for the company and job, or your desire to work for them.

This way, the last thing they see is something positive! Not everyone does this. But I think it's an excellent idea and separates you out in a good way. In other words, you begin your letter on a positive note and end it the same way.

The Resume

A resume provides details about your:

➔ Education
➔ Work history
➔ Abilities and skills that make me want to hire you
➔ Career path or objective

But unlike a cover letter, which has a standardized format, a resume can be formatted in multiple ways. Each format has its own pros and cons to consider. Let's take a look at the various resume types and discuss some of the benefits and disadvantages associated with each one.

The Chronological or Traditional Resume

This is the oldest resume format and is generally used by job hunters who have a great deal of experience. That's because it focuses primarily on your work experience. So the biggest section is your work history. The main reason why interviewers like this format is because it matches your work history to your skills and experience. When looking over your resume, an interviewer can tell exactly where and when you got a particular experience or skill. He or she can also tell how long you've been doing or using it. *Appendix B* gives you an example of a chronological resume.

Here's a sample work history section as it would appear on a chronological resume.

Alaska Airlines	Ticket Agent	8/2004–Present

- Make flight reservations and issued tickets
- Issue boarding passes
- Give fliers departure gate numbers and other important information
- Place destination tags on bags

Sears	Cashier	2/2003–7/2004

- Handled cash, check, and credit card sales
- Ran price checks
- Answered customer questions

As you can see, it tells the employer:

→ The places where you've worked
→ Information about your job duties or responsibilities
→ The dates when you worked at each job

Underneath each job, they'll be a listing of your responsibilities for that one. This is the *matching* I described earlier. By looking at this resume, an interviewer can tell where and when you worked and exactly what you did. Everything's all nice and neat in one place under work history. Remember this so you can see how things differ when we discuss the other resume types.

The Functional or Skills-Based Resume

This is used mainly by job seekers having little or no practical experience. For example, a student who's never worked before. It's also used by people who change fields and don't have much experience in the new one. For instance, someone who's worked mainly in accounting and now wants to move into the travel industry.

But unlike the chronological, the main focus here is on your capabilities, not work history. So the largest section is your skills and abilities rather than your work experience. The biggest problem is that it doesn't match your work history to your capabilities. An employer has to either look at other parts of your resume trying to figure it out or ask you during an interview. *Appendix C* gives you a sample functional resume.

Let's see how the work history section on a functional resume would appear.

| Alaska Airlines | Ticket Agent | 8/2004–Present |
| Sears | Cashier | 2/2003–7/2004 |

Do you see any details about what you did on the job? No. All you see is the company, job title, and dates, nothing more! This is why some employers don't like the functional resume. It doesn't tell me anything about what you did on the job. In order for me to learn about your responsibilities, I have to ask. This takes both time and effort on my part. Some will make the effort; others will not.

Another difference is the location of your work history section. On a chronological, it's near the top and fills most of the space. That's because it provides details about each job. But on a functional, it's near the bottom and uses much less space. All it shows is where and when you worked and your job title or specialty area. The majority of the functional resume is used to highlight your capabilities. The very last thing an employer will see is your lack of work experience. This is how it de-emphasizes your work history.

At the top is where you focus on your capabilities. Here's an example of how that would look:

SKILLS AND ABILITIES

- Extremely good at providing quality customer service
- Highly dependable, organized, and responsible
- Successfully resolved problems and answered questions
- Knowledge of Microsoft Word, Excel, and Outlook

The philosophy behind the functional resume is that your having a great deal of needed and important skills compensates for your lack of practical experience. So concentrating more on what you are capable of doing makes you look pretty impressive. Because of this, matching where and when you got a particular skill doesn't seem all that important. What's important is you are a very capable person with lots of needed skills!

The Combination Resume

This format mixes the chronological and functional resumes together. People generally choose it for the same reasons as the functional. It provides details about your job responsibilities just like a chronological. So the work history section looks similar to a chronological. However, it may contain fewer details because of limited space. But it does provide some details!

This allows an interviewer to do some partial matching of your skills and abilities to experience. *Appendix D* provides a sample combination resume. Here's a sample of how the work history section would look:

Alaska Airlines	**Ticket Agent**	**8/2004–Present**

- Make flight reservations and issued tickets
- Issue boarding passes
- Give fliers departure gate numbers and other important information

Sears	**Cashier**	**2/2003–7/2004**

- Handled cash, check, and credit card sales
- Ran price checks

And like a functional resume, there's a section devoted to your skills and abilities. So the combination resume has two main sections:

→ One highlighting your skills and capabilities (*functional*)
→ The other focusing on your work history (*chronological*)

Which section should come first is totally up to you. Most experts I've read or heard suggest putting your skills first. That's because you want to emphasize what you can, or are capable of doing. I tend to agree with them on this point, although there may be cases where you want to switch the order. It all depends upon how much practical work experience you have.

→ If you believe you have enough to convince an employer to call you in for an interview, then putting your *work history* up top and *capabilities* below it may work best
→ If you don't feel you have enough experience to convince an employer to call you in for an interview, then putting your *capabilities* up top and *work history* below it may work best

In other words, there's no rule governing which comes first and what goes second because each applicant's background is different. But generally-speaking, most decide to put their skills and abilities first.

Tip #1:   Try it both ways and see which one gets the better response

If you're not sure which way to go, I suggest creating two resumes. Send different versions to different employers and see which one gets you more contacts. Then stick with the one that worked best! Just be sure to track which version went to which employer so you can tell which version worked best.

The Electronic, Scannable, or E-Resume

These are all names given to a resume having just plain text and no formatting. That means no bold, italics, underlining, fancy fonts, bullets, numbering, borders, etc. All your information gets electronically put into a searchable database allowing employers to find candidates who meet specific criteria by entering keywords. For example, I can search for applicants who have three or more years experience and a college degree. It's also used for posting resumes to some online job boards.

I suggest substituting *asterisks* or *dashes* in place of bullets or numbering. *Asterisks* might be better only because it's easier for you to see, which makes correcting errors and updating information quicker. *Dashes* tend to blend-in more with your text and get lost in the crowd. Company names should be separated from titles and dates by using *commas*.

Tip #2:   You can make it as long as you wish!

A mistake some applicants make is limiting the information to what's on their paper resumes. Why is this a mistake? Because they fail to realize that electronic resumes aren't meant to be read or viewed by human eyes. They are used for database entry. Paper resumes are limited in size, but electronic ones aren't! This means you can expand on, or add to information already on your resume. I suggest using that extra space to further highlight your capabilities, and/or include some keywords you think a prospective employer may use when searching. This can improve your changes of getting hits, meaning showing-up when the employer runs searches.

Now that we've learned about the different resume types, it's time to focus on what information goes on a resume. No matter which type you choose, the information that goes on it is basically the same. Here are the main sections found on all resumes:

Personal Data

This is where you'd put your contact information:

→ Name
→ Address
→ Phone
→ E-mail

Tip #3:   Your name should be large and preferably bolded!

I've seen this mistake made in plenty of books and by countless job seekers. They'll use a 10 to 12 point font for their names and no bolding. It's a mistake in my opinion because the employer needs to clearly see who's information this is. Employers are busy and can get tons of resumes—hundreds or even thousands! Yours can very easily get lost in the shuffle if your name is too small. Or if it looks like the rest of the text.

But making your name larger, and preferably bolded, is a great way to make your resume standout from others. When someone flips through their stack of resumes, a bigger and bolder name will immediately catch that person's attention. So I suggest making the font size between 16 and 24 point.

And only do this for your name, *not* your address, phone, or e-mail! In other words, the largest thing on your resume should be your name! That's so the employer and interviewer knows who's resume it is.

Tip #4:   When listing your e-mail address, *don't* have it as a hyperlink. A hyperlink means someone can click on it and e-mail software will open.

Typing an e-mail address using Microsoft Word will automatically make it hyperlink. For example, typing ronauerbach@yahoo.com. When it prints out, the blue e-mail address will appear "grayish" on a black and white printer. An employer may notice that difference in font color, which wouldn't make you look good. Just imagine sending a letter to a customer and including your e-mail address that way. An employer might also click on it by accident, which can be very annoying! You want it to be just plain text. So how do you fix it?

Tip #5:   In Microsoft Word, *right-click* on the e-mail address. This will display a menu. *Left-click* the option to remove the hyperlink. Your text will change from blue and underlined, to black without underlining.

Career Objective (*Optional*)

Many suggest putting this on your resume to tell an employer what you're looking for; others say no. Which way you go is a personal choice. For example, suppose you want a front desk job in a hotel. An objective saying this tells an employer you wouldn't be interested in a banquet job. If you're looking for part-time work, your objective can say this. Now an employer knows you aren't interested in full-time positions. So an objective can be useful in telling an employer what kind of work you are seeking.

But a common mistake by applicants is having a more broad rather than specific objective. For example:

1. To obtain a position at a stable and growing company
2. Seeking a position that allows me to use my customer service skills
3. Interested in obtaining a position that utilizes my skills and offers room for growth
4. Looking for a position that uses my extensive sales and marketing background

The problem with objectives like these is they don't really narrow things down for an employer. In other words, they're givens.

➔ Doesn't everyone want a job with potential for growth and career advancement?
➔ Who doesn't want a job that uses our skills and education?
➔ Don't we all want a job at a company that'll stay in business?

So I feel objectives like these *waste* valuable space! I suggest replacing them with something that tells an employer what you can do. In other words, add or expand upon your skills, education, and/or work history. Now you're using that wasted space for something that will make you look even more impressive. Something that further improves chances of gaining an interview.

Better objectives, in my opinion, would be something like:

1. Interested in obtaining a travel and tourism internship
2. Looking for a position as a management trainee
3. Seeking employment as a Biotech Engineer
4. To obtain a part-time position working in the healthcare field

These are more effective because they tell an employer exactly what you want. They're not broad, but rather more specific. Objectives like these actually help an employer get a better sense of what you're seeking. They also make you look good because you're showing a clear sense of direction and career path.

For example:

→ The travel objective specifies the candidate is looking for an *internship*. Now the employer knows he or she isn't interested in a permanent full or part-time job. The applicant is merely attempting to get some experience in the field.

→ The engineering objective mentions a very specific job, *Biotech Engineer*. If I think this person may be suited for a Chemical Engineer position I happen to have, I know he or she wouldn't be interested.

Tip #6:   I generally suggest having no objective on your resume

The reason is because I think it's best to leave all your options open! Employers are very good at matching applicants with positions. They may even have another job you're unaware of that's perfect for you. For example, a position that isn't advertised yet or is in another department.

What if they contact you with a job that doesn't interest you? Simple, politely thank them and let them know it's not what you're looking for. This is something they'll respect and admire. And that makes you look extremely good! It's also something they might remember the next time a position becomes available. My point is that leaving it up to the employer to decide what you're qualified for can often result in greater opportunities.

Education

This is where you'd list any degrees, certificates, and other relevant training you have. A common mistake is to assume you wouldn't include on-the-job training or other non-school training. Wrong! Education means gaining knowledge. It doesn't matter if it's a workshop, college, an in-house training seminar, certification class, DVD, etc.

→ Any and all forms of training = education = expanded knowledge!

This means you can lump everything together in this one section. Now some do choose to separate them by adding another section for their specialized training. That's to draw more attention to your training in a particular area.

In computers for example, there are various certifications, such as: MCSE, A+, MCSD, CNE, and Linux. In human resources, there are certifications like PHR, SPHR, and CPP. Listing these under education is fine. But if you want to draw more attention to your having a particular or multiple certifications, then you may want to put them under a section called *Certifications*.

If you work in sales and attended a series of workshops in cold-calling techniques, marketing strategies, and new products or services, you might add a section called *Sales and Marketing Training*. Doing this will draw more attention to your having sales training.

Whether or not you choose to lump all your education and training into a single education section, or separate them out is totally up to you. My point is: Be sure you include any and all training that you feel is relevant to the job or profession! The key word here is *relevant*. That means it has to be something that would impress an interviewer.

Work History

As I mentioned earlier, this section is the primary focus of a *chronological* resume. Now a common mistake is to list every job you've had. You should only list only the ones relevant in some way to the kind of work you're seeking. This means sifting through your various jobs to decide which ones to include, and which to exclude.

Another mistake is to list every assignment from an employment agency or temporary service (temp service). This makes your resume look rather messy and unprofessional in my opinion. So let me suggest a better way to organize things.

Tip #7: Group multiple agency assignments together. For example:

Adams & Associates	**Various**	**10/2005–3/2006**
<ul><li>Was sent by the agency on multiple assignments</li><li>Worked as a Receptionist handling 15 phone lines with 20 extensions</li><li>Typed letters and updated databases</li></ul>		

Adams & Associates is the employment agency that sent you to other companies. Notice how the job title says *Various*. This says you had multiple jobs. For example, you may have worked one day as a Receptionist and another as a Customer Service Representative. What you do here is list any relevant job duties from all your different assignments. Doing this makes your resume look cleaner, and neatness counts! If you don't like the word *various*, you can use *multiple*.

How do you list multiple assignments through different agencies? That's a very good question. Many people, including myself, have used multiple agencies during the same period of time. We do this to increase the number of work assignments and/or work in a wider variety of companies or fields. Well the answer is to group those assignments and agencies together in a single listing. An example of this is shown below:

Various	Various	2006

- Was sent by the agency on multiple assignments
- Worked as a Receptionist handling 15 phone lines with 20 extensions
- Typed letters and updated databases

The word *Various* in both the company name and job title tells me you worked at multiple places and held different jobs. Employers realize how common it is for people to work through multiple agencies. So your doing this won't make you look bad at all.

Besides, the more agencies you deal with, the more potential assignments you can get. This shows wise decision-making and a strong desire to want to work! Once again, you can substitute the word *multiple* for *various* because they mean the same thing. Or use one for the employer's name and the other for the assignments you've had.

If you worked at a particular assignment for a long period of time—several weeks or months—then you could list it under the company name instead of the agency. For instance:

Home Depot	Office Manager	2006

- Filled cash register drawers with cash for transactions
- Prepared and printed management reports, such as Profit and Loss
- Processed timesheets and payroll

Technically, you were employed by the agency. But working at Home Depot all those weeks or months is long enough for them to vouch for the quality of your work. So there's nothing wrong with listing them on your resume instead of the agency. The decision to list it this way is your choice.

Tip #8:   Employers like numbers!

Let's assume you're applying for a job as a Department Manager and have the following job duty listed on your resume:

→ Directly responsible for the budget and all sales

The way it's currently written isn't bad since you do mention your being responsible for the budget and sales. That's very good and impressive. But you don't indicate how large a budget you handle. Nor tell me how much is generated by sales. So an interviewer doesn't know if you're handling small, mid-size, or large figures.

In other words, there is a difference between someone who manages a $1 million budget and another who only manages a $50,000 budget. Or someone who handles $500,000 in sales versus another who handles $5 million. While both are doing essentially the same job, the amounts involved are quite different. Now consider these possible rewrites:

→ Directly responsible for a $10 million budget and sales totaling $150 million
→ Directly responsible for a $200,000 budget and $1.4 million in sales
→ Directly responsible for a $50,000 budget and sales totaling $375,000

Each of these revisions say basically the same thing. You are directly responsible for the budget and level of sales. But unlike the original way, these revised ones provide more details. They include amounts for how much the budget and sales are. In business, many interviewers like having numbers in there and actually prefer it. That's because he or she can tell whether you have handled the level needed for the job.

For example, if the job requires someone capable of managing a $3 million budget, will an applicant who's only managed $150,000 be able to handle it? Some interviewers might say yes because budgeting is budgeting. Others may say the discrepancy is just too great. In other words, an amount too far below what the job demands isn't good enough. So which way should you go when putting your resume together? Well that's strictly a personal choice. But I suggest putting any numbers you feel will impress an employer just enough to call you in for an interview.

For example, if a job is looking for a person to supervise 300 people and you've only supervised 15, then leaving the number off might be better. That's because your experience in this area is very far below what they're looking for. If the job doesn't indicate how many people you'd be supervising, then it's a purely a judgment call.

But as I've told countless job seekers before, if you leave it off and an employer really wants to know, then they'll have to contact you and ask. That's the ultimate goal with any resume—to be contacted by an employer! So I say a little mystery can sometimes work in your favor. That's because if an employer really wants to know, then they'll have no choice but to ask you directly.

Tip #9:   How you format dates can make a big difference!

Take a good look at this person's work history.

4/2007–7/2007	**Cashier**	**Safeway Food & Drugs**
▪ Rang-up customer sales ▪ Did price checks ▪ Handled returns and exchanges ▪ Assisted customers in finding products		

As you can see, this person worked as a Cashier for around three months. Now suppose this person wants to find another job that involves cashiering. Does this person have enough experience? One interviewer may feel three months is enough; another may say it's too little. But what can be done? After all, you don't want to lie!

Well here's a neat little trick. Instead of having the months and years when you worked on your resume, just put the years. This way, the employer will think you have more experience than you really do. On a job application, you'd put your months and years of employment. But on a resume, it's not required. So you have tremendous flexibility in how you decide to list your employment dates!

Let's see how this resume would look using my little trick.

2007	Cashier	Safeway Food & Drugs

- Rang-up customer sales
- Did price checks
- Handled returns and exchanges
- Assisted customers in finding products

How much work experience does this Cashier now have? It doesn't say exactly how many days, weeks, or months. But many would just assume you worked the entire year. So you've turned your three months of experience into a year!

Can you be held responsible if an employer made an incorrect assumption? No. If they really wanted to know how much, they could've looked at your application or asked you. So you didn't lie; they made a false assumption. But once you have your foot in the door, you can then show what a fully-capable individual you are. So this little trick is a way of remaining honest and playing into the inherent assumption of an employer or interviewer.

Tip #10: There is a way to deal with periods of unemployment

Some of you may have large or several small gaps in your work history. And this sometimes raises a red flag to employers. A spotty work record could indicate you're a problem employee who's incapable of holding onto a job for long. Or you just don't know what you want to do. Or maybe you're somebody who really doesn't want to work and would rather have fun. Interviewers don't want to hire people like this. But there are legitimate reasons for large or multiple gaps in employment. Maybe you:

→ Moved and needed time to get settled and look for work
→ Took time off to raise a family
→ Went back to school and decided to focus on your studies
→ Had a family emergency that prevented you from working
→ Were in an major accident or hospitalized for a period of time
→ Were laid-off, outsourced, or downsized and needed to retrain
→ Were on-strike and out walking the picket line

Would you put any of these on your resume? Well there are some who say to do it. However, I don't feel you should and here's why. They're interview questions! You need to explain in person or over the phone, your reason(s) for the gap(s). Putting it on you resume doesn't give you the chance to really explain. Or allow the interviewer to probe deeper. So I say to leave these off!

Instead, you can list the cities and states where you worked. In other words, *substitute* them for your dates of employment. Doing this will make it appear you were steadily working because I'll assume you were. Once again, you're playing into the inherent assumption of an employer that people want to work. Here's how my suggestion would look on a chronological resume:

Kmart	Customer Service	Bellevue, WA

- Assisted customers in finding the right product
- Stocked shelves and put prices on merchandise
- Answered customer questions
- Helped direct customers

Albertsons	Stocker	Seattle, WA

- Stocked shelves
- Did inventory counts

Notice how this resume doesn't have any dates. If an interviewer wants to know when you worked, he or she has to ask. And that's exactly what you want! When you're contacted for an interview and your employment history comes up, that's when you'll explain your employment gap(s). And when you complete job applications, you'll put your reason(s) on there. This way, you look qualified and impress me! Just realize that some employers may not contact you due to the lack of dates. It's a risk you'll have to take. But take comfort in knowing that many other will contact and hire you!

If your gap was due to schooling, then you don't have to hide the dates unless you choose to. The reason is because when I look at your resume, I'll see your school dates and realize you were attending school. This counters the assumption you were simply goofing off and not productive.

You weren't goofing off and were productive. It's just you weren't working, but rather getting trained. So you still look good. Remember, training = expanded knowledge. And that's always a good thing to interviewers! So I would suggest having dates on there. But the choice is strictly up to you.

Tip #11: You can also use this technique even if you don't have employment gaps!

Why would you do this? Because it leaves a little mystery with the big question, "When did you work in those jobs? " In order for an employer to find out, they'll have to contact you and ask. So you could deliberately leave dates off as a way to increase your chances of being contacted. Once again, some may be leery, but many others will ask. My suggestion is to leave your dates on there. That's only because you've got a steady work history so there's no reason to hide them. However, the decision is yours to make. I just threw it up as a possibility you may want to consider.

Skills and Abilities

This section highlights what you can do or offer an employer, and fills the majority of a *functional* resume. It's a bulleted list of your skills and abilities. For example:

Skills and Abilities

- Ability to provide quality customer service
- Strong organizational skills
- Created a variety of reports and spreadsheets
- Knowledge of MS Word, Excel, and Outlook

Some lump all their various skills together in one section. Others have multiple sections with each focusing on a particular type of skill. For example:

Computer Skills

- Microsoft Windows, Word, Excel, and PowerPoint
- Internet and E-mail

Office Skills

- Extremely well-organized and responsible
- Customer-service orientated
- Highly motivated and a team-player
- Excellent communication skills

Leadership and Managerial Skills

- Managed a team of 300
- Increased profits by 18%
- Actively handled accounts valued at $1 million
- Am a strong decision-maker and leader
- Successfully motivate employees to meet or exceed goals

Grouping your skills by category or type can make it easier for an employer to focus on a particular area. It can also break the resume into blocks of information rather than one big listing. Both ways essentially contain the same information. It's just a matter of how it's presented. I've used both and have been successful. So which way you go is up to you.

References (*Optional*)

This section lists contact information for people who can say what a good employee you'd make. It would have their names, job titles, relationship to you, phone number, and address. Most resumes don't include this unless an employer asks for it. References often aren't checked until you're either very close to getting the job or have actually started. So I suggest leaving this section off your resume unless an employer asks for it. Instead, put your references on a separate sheet that you can provide when needed.

Tip #12: Putting *References available upon request* is also unnecessary

Are you going to say no if asked for references? Of course not. So it's a given! Use this space for something more important to helping you get the job. For example, include another skill or expand something already on your resume.

PART 2:

Interview Types

This section discusses the various kinds of interviews you may encounter during your job search. Whether or not you will actually run into all of these is impossible for anybody to say. But my philosophy is this: *Be prepared for anything an interviewer may throw at you*!

The reason is because a large part of successful interviewing is not being caught totally off-guard. So preparing in advance for different interviewing situations will help you relax more and handle it well when and if the time comes. Furthermore, your competition may not have anticipated that particular interview format. Your being ready for it may be just enough for you to handle it better and walk out the winner!

We'll learn about the following types of interviews:

1. Face-to-Face
2. Meal
3. Phone
4. Group
5. Computer-Based
6. Hands-on or Project

Face-to-Face Interview

This type of interview is the traditional or standard format. You're being interviewed one-on-one by a single interviewer in the interviewer's office, conference room, or some other quiet spot.

Because this is the most common interviewing method, most applicants are prepared for it. That means your competition will be ready. But it doesn't automatically mean they will do well! Why? Because they may not behave in the right way. It's not enough to simply respond well to the interviewer's questions. You also need to behave in the proper manner. This means both your answers and body language must be at the top of their game. In this section, we'll focus on your body language and overall attitude. In the next, we'll concentrate on how to answer the questions. This way, you'll be fully-prepped and ready for interviews!

> **KEY #1:** Relax!

Interviewers understand that it's very common for an applicant to be somewhat nervous and scared. After all, you're in a room by yourself with nobody else but this stranger you have to get through in order to get that job. Who wouldn't be nervous in this situation? The important thing is the *degree* of nervousness you show! A little is all right, but you don't want to be:

- Shaking like a leaf
- Fidgeting with your hands
- Shaking your foot or leg up and down
- Constantly moving your head back and forth
- Waving your hands around.

Doing any of these during an interview is generally taken as a sign of extreme nervousness, so beware of them. I suggest practicing in front of a mirror or having somebody to pretend to interview you. Don't dwell on the answers you give, concentrate on your body language. In other words, look to see if you're doing any of the things I've listed. If so, then try to minimize or eliminate them. This often isn't very easy! To help combat your nervousness, there are some things you can do:

- Realize you're not along in being scared or nervous. Your competition is too!
- Take a few deep breaths prior to your interview to help yourself relax, but do it in a more private area. In other words, you don't want the interviewer or a Receptionist seeing it. They *must* see you more relaxed! So I suggest doing it in your car, a restroom, or anywhere outside the office.
- Know you'll try your best to do well, which is the most anybody can hope for
- Say to yourself, "I'm ready for this and will try my best!"

➜ Have all your interviewing materials ready ahead of time so you won't have do any last-minute running around. I've known people who've waited until the last-minute and couldn't find something important. That increases the pressure and only makes you more nervous!

KEY #2:   How you handshake is very important

Shaking hands with somebody may seem like the easiest and most natural thing in the world. Yet many job seekers don't do it properly and struggle with it. Men will sometimes have a very firm and bone-crushing grip that can actually hurt or feel as though something's going to break. For women, the handshake tends to be the exact opposite. They'll sometimes have one that's very loose and limp like a blade of grass blowing in the wind.

A proper handshake needs to be firm, yet not crushingly so. It also needs to signal confidence and a sense that you are a business professional who can handle the job. So you need a grip that's both firm enough to signal confidence and pride, yet soft enough to be professional and not feel like it'll hurt. In other words, the manner in which you shake hands is important to success and forms an early impression of you as a professional.

Whenever you shake hands, you should never wildly swing your arms up and down. People will sometimes do this as a sign of nervousness or a way of to appear more friendly. You can't loose sight you are in an interview and must always behave like a true professional. So your handshake should be a more natural and business-like motion.

You also don't want to shake too many times where the interviewer begins to think, "Enough already with the shaking, let's move on." Or use both hands to shake. In some countries, that is an acceptable way to greet people, but not in the United States. It's the same thing with kissing on both cheeks. In some countries, that's how they show respect and greet somebody, but not here in the U.S. You need to show an awareness of how things are done in this country!

KEY #3:   When speaking, look the interviewer in the eye

Another sign of nervousness or being scared is not looking someone in the eye when speaking to him or her. During your interview, it's very important to look directly at the interview while you're speaking. This shows you're unafraid, confident, and professional! For instance, looking down in your lap while talking about yourself doesn't come across as very believable. An interviewer will think, "If you really believe what you're telling me and are professional, you'd be looking right at me." In other words, looking away is taken as either:

➜ You're very nervous and afraid
➜ You've got something to hide
➜ You're lying
➜ You wrote down your exact words and can't think on your feet

It's often these little things that can make a big difference during an interview! That's why you must concentrate on them just as much as you do with your answers. So make sure you look directly at the interviewer while speaking. Yet don't stare so intently that you appear as though your eyes are burning right through someone. This is the sort of cold, hard stare that serial or stone-cold killers will tend to have.

In situations like being behind bars or a member of a gang, this type of look is used for survival. It sends the message that I'm not afraid and "Don't mess with me!" But when it comes to interviewing, that look can really frighten an interviewer. He or she may be deftly afraid of you and want to leave right away. So if you have a look that comes across this way, you better adjust it before you go on any interviews!

Now this isn't often easy for those who've been in prison for a long while. When your daily routine is looking more cold and tough, it can literally become natural and a part of you. So the adjustment may be harder to make. But many people have done it and I'm confident that with some practice, you can too!

Tip #1: It's all right to look away when showing the interviewer something

There maybe times when you need to look away from the interviewer. For example, if you brought something to show the interviewer and are discussing it, then you may have to look at it from time-to-time. You're looking at it might direct the interviewer's attention to it as well.

You can also use your hands to accomplish this. For example, not only can I look at what I brought, but I can use my hand to direct the interviewer's attention to it. Now you don't want to simply throw it on the interviewer's desk. That's a common mistake because you're presuming the interviewer wants to see it. Maybe he or she does, but then again, perhaps not. You want to take it out and show it to him or her as if you were in a business meeting discussing something. In other words, it should be a very natural motion and not a throw it at me one. You could either:

➔ Hold it up in the air and direct his or her attention to parts of it or the whole thing. If the interviewer wants to look at it more closely, then you can either lean in or hand it to him or her. But don't get up and stand behind the interviewer. You're a stranger and it's unprofessional behavior at this point. It's all right too lean in and point to things, but you should not stand up and encroach upon one's personal space. If you choose to hand it to the interviewer rather than leaning in, then I suggest having a copy for yourself to refer to while discussing it. That shows advanced preparation and foresight.

➔ Ask the interviewer if he or she would mind your showing something. That way, you're asking for permission before taking it out. Sometimes an interviewer will deny your request because time is limited. If that's the case, then comply willingly. If you're given permission, then go right ahead and show it.

KEY #4: Samples of past work can prove success!

A very common mistake is not having anything concrete to show the interviewer. Quite often, an applicant will simply discuss what he or she has done, but won't have anything to really back it up. So it's up to the interviewer to decide whether he or she is telling the truth and can really do it.

But having something concrete that an interviewer can see and touch is much better. That's because you're proving your ability to do it! So it's no longer your word, but rather hard evidence. In an interview, this carries tremendous weight and can make a huge positive impression! It not only demonstrates exactly what you are capable of doing, but also shows advanced preparation.

Tip #2:   Bring samples of your best work

Some applicants make a mistake by bringing something that isn't really all that good. It may look good on the surface, yet filled with errors in spelling, grammar, formatting, etc. So just because it may visually look nice doesn't automatically mean an interviewer will be impressed. Be prepared for the interviewer to really look at it! In other words, an interviewer may not just glance at it, but actually read it carefully. So whatever you bring, it must be relevant, impressive, and error-free!

For example, if you're interviewing for an Administrative Assistant position, you can bring part of a report you're proud of and either put together or helped create. Or the master document you created in order to do a mail-merge with the various merge fields on it. If you are interviewing for a Sales Manager position, you can bring a proposal you put together or worked on. Or maybe an advertising pitch or marketing strategy you developed to increase business.

Tip #3:   It's better to allow the interviewer to keep a copy

Many applicants will bring examples, but only to look at right then and there. So the interviewer isn't able to keep one for review or to show others when discussing your candidacy. This is a mistake in my professional opinion. I feel it's best to allow the interviewer to keep a copy because it's something that can always be referred back to when discussing your candidacy. In other words, instead of just having my interview notes to look over, I'll have something more concrete to prove your ability to do good work. This keeps you fresher in my mind and can make you standout more than others!

Now there may be times when you prefer an interviewer not keep a copy of something. Suppose you're an art student who's drawn something on one of those huge portfolio pads. I can understand why you might not want an interviewer retaining a copy. But I also think you have alternatives to work around this.

It certainly wouldn't make sense to tear your drawing out of your portfolio and give it to the interviewer. But you could easily make a copy of it on smaller paper, which could then be handed over. In other words, snap a picture of it and either give the interviewer the photograph or a copy printed on paper. That way, the interviewer will have something and your original is fully-intact and in your possession. If there are several drawings, then you could take a picture of one of them and give it to the interviewer shortly after your interview. This way, you won't need to copy everything in your portfolio. All I'm saying is to give the interviewer at least one sample to prove your ability to do solid work.

But what if your main concern is giving the interviewer something that's original work? In other words, you're worried about your original design being out of your control. Well that's perfectly understandable. Nobody wants to run the risk of having their original idea, music, or work stolen. The problem is you're lack of trust.

If you're willing to work for a company and give them personal data like your date of birth and Social Security Number, then you should trust them not to steal your original work. An interviewer isn't looking to steal from you, he or she is simply deciding whether to hire you. But if you're that concerned about it, then you could protect yourself ahead of time with things like copyrights, trademarks, or patents. This way, if something was actually stolen, then you have legal recourse to deal with it.

Tip #4:   Hide anything confidential or for internal use only!

Another common mistake is for an applicant to give something to an interviewer that really should have been kept confidential. Interviewers are business men and women, so you must always treat them as such. That means protecting information by not revealing anything that really shouldn't be seen by outsiders.

So if you're going to show or give the interviewer something with confidential information on it, make sure you blank out things like:

➔ Social Security and account numbers
➔ Customer names and addresses
➔ Bank account or financial information

Assuming you don't want to ruin your original(s), I suggest making a copy. Use a thick black marker to cross-out anything the interviewer shouldn't really see on the copy you just made.

Tip #5:   *Don't* give this copied one to the interviewer!

One reason is because we can sometimes hold it up to the light or flip it over and see what was crossed out. So make sure you darkened everything well-enough and then make your copy. This will help darken it further, prevent any ink from rubbing-off in the interviewer's hands, and further protect anything confidential.

Tip #6:   You may have to copy things multiple times

I've sometimes had to redo the copy I just made because some confidential information was slightly visible. That means using the marker on the copy and then recopying it until that information is no longer visible. Just be aware of this when you make your copies.

The bottom-line with face-to-face interviews is knowing they are the most common way to interview somebody. It's perfectly natural and expected to be somewhat nervous, but you don't want to be overly nervous. I suggest having someone pretend to interview you and watch your body language. Review how you did and look for ways to improve!

Meal Interview

Here's a format you may never have encountered. It's not quite as common as the face-to-face, but is gaining in popularity. So I suggest being more prepared for it, especially with sales positions. The reason is because salespeople may be out in the field and might schedule interviews at places like coffeehouses or a local eatery. I've witnessed plenty of interviews happening around me while sitting at places like *Barnes & Noble* and *Starbucks*. Or a meal interview can happen in the company's own lunchroom in a more private and quiet section.

The reason meal interviews are an excellent way to see how well an applicant may fit-in is because the interviewer will get to see you in a more relaxing atmosphere. He or she can also picture you in a business meeting, luncheon, holiday party, etc. So the interviewer can not only ask you questions in a more relaxing atmosphere, but can also see how you may behave in a more social setting.

Now as an applicant, you may be saying that you'll do much better here because the pressure's off and you can feel more at home. But it's exactly that kind of attitude that can literally doom you!

KEY #1:   Don't relax too much!

The main reason interviewers like meal interviews is that applicants will often drop or lower their guard. This means an applicant could say things he or she wouldn't have ordinarily mentioned in a more pressured or traditional interview format. Don't fall for this!

You must always remember that you are being interviewed. The only difference is how and where your interview is being conducted. So don't lower or drop your guard. Also remain full-aware of what you're saying and how you're acting. In other words, think and act in the same way as if this was a face-to-face interview.

KEY #2:   Watch your eating and drinking habits

I've seen many applicants order high-priced meals because an interviewer will often say you can order whatever you like. But this is a classic mistake in my professional opinion because you are taking advantage of the interviewer's generosity! You are interviewing for a job and are already costing me big bucks is what the interviewer will be thinking. In other words, you haven't even been hired yet and are already taking advantage of me. This doesn't remotely make you look good! So don't over-spend.

Another mistake applicants will make is ordering something rather messy. In other words, something like a cheeseburger with everything. Now this isn't overly expensive, but it can be very messy to eat. Just imagine the impression you'll send by:

→ Getting something like ketchup or mustard on your clothes, or worse, splattering it onto the interviewer. Even if you cover yourself with a napkin, liquids can still bleed through and leave a mark.

→ Getting crumbs all over the place and making a huge mess. Perhaps getting some of them onto the interviewer's documents. Picture him or her going back to the office or on to the next interview with crumbs falling out. Would that make the interviewer look very business-like?

→ Talking with your mouth still full of food. Perhaps spitting pieces of it out as you speak.

→ Reaching for documents like your resume or shaking the interviewer's hand while your hands are still a bit wet or greasy.

→ Having bad or hot breath from eating things like onions, peppers, or jalapeños.

Not the best way to impress and entice an interviewer to consider you for employment! Also not the type of things an applicant would normally think about when preparing for interviews. But this is exactly what an interviewer will be focusing on! So I suggest you order something that's not as messy. Maybe passing on the onions, mustard, and ketchup. Or perhaps getting a salad or something you can eat with a knife and fork instead of just using your hands.

When it comes to drinking, you need to be even more careful! Here are some helpful suggestions and things to watch-out for:

→ *Never* order an alcoholic beverage! This is highly inappropriate and gets you off on the wrong foot. Besides, it opens the door to an interviewer wondering if you have a drinking problem. This is an interview and not a social event!

→ Don't get a very large drink. This is similar to ordering a very expensive meal. If the interviewer is buying, then you are taking advantage of his or her generosity. That doesn't make a good first impression! But even if bought your own drink, it's still not a good idea. Interviews are relatively short and so a gigantic drink isn't necessary. An interviewer may also picture your having 5, 6, 7 cups of coffee throughout the day, which isn't a good impression. Or worse, he or she may wonder if you have an addiction or drinking problem.

→ Be sure not to spill things. If you are getting something where you can put a lid on it, do it! Even if you wouldn't ordinarily do that, it's a good idea. The last thing you want is to spill anything on yourself or on the interviewer. So it's good business practice and manners. If you can't put a lid on it, then don't have it filled to the very top. Leave some room for it to slosh around. I've seen applicants spill their drinks on the way to the table, which is very embarrassing!

The bottom-line is that meal interviews can be very tough. It's because you have to focus on your answers to the interviewer's questions and watch your body language. At the same time, being aware of your eating and drinking habits. What makes this tough is we don't normally concentrate on all this simultaneously. So it's not something we're accustomed to doing.

But when it comes to successfully handling a meal interview, it's super important! It may be a good idea to practice by having somebody pretend to interview you at a local restaurant or coffee house. Have that person focus on your eating and drinking habits. Then review and look for things that could be improved or should have been avoided or minimized.

Phone Interview

A phone is exactly what it sounds like. You receive a phone call and have your interview. Sometimes, phone interviews are setup in advance so you know when it's going to be. Other times, the phone suddenly rings and off goes your interview.

So part of what makes them tough is the fact they can happen whenever! If you know it's coming, then you have time to prepare and get everything ready so you can do your best. But if you're caught by surprise, then you may not be thinking as clearly nor have everything handy. But there are ways to successfully handle them and be ready at all times.

> **KEY #1**:   Phone interviews are mainly for screening purposes

Most times, a phone interview isn't nearly as in-depth as the other interview formats. Interviewers are busy and generally don't have lots of time to spend on the phone. He or she will also be unable to gauge your body language and facial expressions because you can only be heard and not seen. As I've mentioned before, body language can reveal a great deal about an applicant. Part of interviewing is listening very carefully to your words, while paying very close attention to your facial expressions and body language. With phone interviews, the facial and body language components are removed because you cannot be seen. All an interviewer has to rely on is what you say and how you sound.

So phone interviews are often used to pre-screen candidates and decide who should be taken to the next level. That would normally be a face-to-face meeting. This means you have a relatively short period of time to impress the interviewer enough to advance. How long? Well that varies, but generally-speaking, phone interviews last around 15 to 20 minutes. This includes the time for both interviewer questions and your own.

> **KEY #2**:   Speak well and with confidence!

Because the interviewer's only impression of you is your phone voice and manner, you must project yourself extremely well. This means speaking:

- ➜ In a voice that's not too soft nor too loud. A soft voice indicates shyness, nervousness, or lack of confidents. A more powerful, yet not super loud voice projects confidence and pride.
- ➜ In a professional manner. A common mistake is to become more relaxed in your tone of voice. The reason is because you may be at home or in a more comfortable environment where the pressure's off. So it's only natural to become more relaxed in the way you sound and behave. Don't fall for this! Remember, this is an interview and so you must be professional and treat it as such. So be more aware of becoming relaxed and more friendly.

Tip #1:   Cell phones aren't the best for phone interviews

Many people today have only a cell phone or mainly use their cell phone as their primary telephone. Now this is all right for non-interviews. But when it comes to interviewing, I suggest having a landline—regular touchtone or dial phone. The reason why I say this is because:

→ Your clarity of voice over a landline is usually better than a cell phone. This means the interviewer will be able to hear you better over a regular phone.

→ Landlines don't get cut-off or interrupted as much as cell phones. Many cordless phones have multiple frequencies from which to choose. This reduces interference and prevents people from being disconnected. Most cell phones don't have this feature and are more subject to atmospheric conditions, leading to disconnects or interruptions.

→ Cell phones tend to be more awkward to hold onto when reaching for documents or writing things down. With a landline, it's much easier to hold onto the phone and do other things. That's because you can always attach a shoulder holder to it, which frees your hands to do other things.

Tip #2:   *Never* put your phone on speaker or speakerphone!

I've known people who've put their phones, whether it's a cell or landline, into speakerphone mode during phone interviews. This is a mistake in my professional opinion. The reason is because you won't sound nearly as clear as you normally would. You'll sound more like you're inside a box with an echo in your voice. This makes it harder for the interviewer to understand you.

Your goal is to be heard very clearly! Remember, you cannot be seen. So the only way an interviewer can evaluate you is through the sound of your voice and your words. Now for those of you where English is a second language, having an accent may be tough to understand. Compound this with a speakerphone, and it's even harder! So you must sound more natural and clear!

Tip #3:   Have your resume by the phone

Because you never know when that phone will ring, the last thing you want to be is totally unprepared or running around looking for your resume. So I suggest keeping a copy near or underneath the phone. This way, you'll be able to refer to it more easily.

Tip #4:   For those of you having multiple versions of your resume

Why would someone have different versions of their resume? One reason is because you may apply for jobs in different fields. Each resume would be molded towards a specific one. Another reason would be if you're applying for jobs involving different levels of responsibility. For instance, if you're applying for support and managerial positions, then you may want one resume tailored for support staff and another geared towards management.

If you do have multiple versions of your resume, I suggest making a copy of each one and clipping them all together. This way, you'll have them all in one spot and won't loose any. Make sure you label each one so you'll know which is which. When your phone rings, it'll be easier to grab the right one without having to run all over the place looking for it.

Tip #5:   Always have pen and paper ready

Another sign of preparation is having a pen or pencil handy, along with a notepad. This way, you'll be ready to take notes during your interview. It'll help you compare this job to any others. It's also helpful when you need to refer back to or clarify something with the interviewer. Furthermore, it shows advanced preparation and good business practices. Lastly, make sure your pen works! I suggest periodically checking and having an extra one just in case. If you'll be using pencil, then have extras just in case the point gets worn or breaks. Also be sure your erasers work and are in good shape. Otherwise, crossing something out and making changes can get rather messy.

You might be thinking these are little things or givens. But you'd be surprised how easily we can forget them when the time comes. Remember, you don't know exactly when that phone is going to ring. You might use them for other things. Or you may put them somewhere else because you needed it at that moment. My point is that it's very easy to forget to check or not have them ready when the time comes. These are the last things you need during a phone interview!

Tip #6:   Keep noise down to a minimum

The ideal is to have a phone in an area where it will be very quiet and you can talk undisturbed. This is so you don't get interrupted and the interviewer can easily hear you. The last thing you want is an interviewer hearing lots of noises or screaming in the background. For example, the kids screaming or crying. Or somebody yelling, "Where's my …!".

Now you may be laughing, but you have to remember that your phone can ring at anytime day or night. It can even ring on weekends! I've known people who've gotten calls early Sunday morning or late Friday night. Recruiters don't' always work 9 to 5 Monday through Friday. In addition, some businesses are open late and/or on weekends. So I say be prepared for that phone to ring 24x7.

Tip #7:   Keep bullet points by the phone

When your phone rings, I suggest having a bulleted list of important things you'd like to mention. This way, you won't have to worry about memory. You may remember it now, but when that phone rings, you might not. This is especially true if you're very busy or stressed-out. But don't write down exactly what you're going to say. Your voice and words need to sound very natural, not scripted or robotic. Bullet your main ideas and thoughts. When the time comes, you'll phrase everything right then and there. This way, you'll get your points across and sound more natural. You'll also show your ability to think on your feet, which is important in the workplace.

Now if you're applying for jobs in different fields and/or various levels of responsibility, then you may want to have individual lists that go with each one. For example, one listing for managerial positions and another for support ones. Or one concentrating on bookkeeping jobs and another focused on general office support. Index cards clipped together can work nicely here. Once again, make sure you label which card goes with which type of jobs. You could also have a piece of paper that's divided into sections that are clearly labeled. This way, you can have one paper that can be used for all the various types of jobs you're applying for. Either way, it's up to you. The main thing is to be highly-organized!

The bottom-line with phone interviews is being prepared for that phone to ring at anytime, day or night. The tips I've given you will make you better-prepared and ready for that phone call. Thus, increasing your chances of success and making you seem more professional!

Group Interview

Group interviews are ones where there's either:

→ Multiple interviewers and one applicant
→ One interviewer and multiple candidates
→ Several interviewers and multiple applicants

Regardless of how group interviews are conducted, the amount of pressure a candidate is subjected to increases. That's because it's no longer a one-on-one situation. There are other people in the same room with you. Depending upon the group format used, your approach will be slightly different. Let's see how by looking at each of the three group formats individually.

Multiple Interviewers and You

This is a situation where you are the only one being interviewed. But instead of having just a single interviewer, there are several. How many isn't important. Quite often, just one interviewer will do all the talking, while the others will remain completely silent. This can be very frustrating to applicants and catches many of them off-guard. But there's a reason for this.

The one who's speaking focuses on the questions to ask, while the rest are evaluating on your responses. In other words, those others aren't distracted by having to think of the next question. They can devote all their efforts to your actual words and body language. So you really need to impress in order to be successful!

A classic mistake applicants will often make is to ignore the ones who aren't speaking. It's not they're being rude, but rather it's human nature to devote more attention to the one speaking. However, this is a business meeting. So you cannot ignore anybody in the room with you!

Not periodically looking over at the silent one(s) is considered very unprofessional and doesn't impress anybody. The interviewers may begin to wonder if you're blind. They'll say to themselves, "Can't you see there are others here with you?" So it's very important to acknowledge their existence by looking directly at each person in the room from time-to-time.

Now you don't want your head swinging from side-to-side constantly as if you're watching a tennis match. It has to be a more natural motion done while you're speaking. So you have to look around at the interviewers while speaking. In a sense, you're multi-tasking because you've got two things to do simultaneously. Being able to juggle multiple things at one time is very important in the workplace. That ability is partly being tested right here.

Multiple Applicants and One Interviewer

Let's now focus on your being interviewed along with other candidates by a single interviewer. This situation is the exact opposite from what we just discussed above. This time, you're in a room with others who want the exact same job as you. Many applicants will feel increased pressure here because they're surrounded by their competition. That's because each candidate is trying to outshine the others. Whether or not the pressure really is greater is a matter of personal opinion. However, many do feel it more when put inside a room with their competitors.

Yet it can very advantageous for a job seeker to be placed in this situation! The reason is because you can learn a great deal about your fellow applicants. Something you just can't do if it was only you in that room! Here, you get to meet them and listen to what their backgrounds and qualifications are. You also get a better sense of how you measure-up in comparison. So even though the degree of nervousness and pressure increases, there are huge benefits to it.

Tip #1: Listen very carefully to what your fellow candidates say

Listen carefully to see how well they communicate and respond to the questions. Focus your attention on their backgrounds, including their levels of education, work history and years of experience, on-the-job experiences and training, etc. This way, you'll get a good sense of how you compare and more importantly, how you differ!

Here are some things you should focus on and take note of as your interview progresses.

→ Areas where you *exceed* your competition. When it's your turn to speak, be sure you mention them.

→ Instance(s) where you believe they made any mistakes or errors. For example, did somebody stumble when they spoke? Did someone not fully-answer the interviewer's question? Did a candidate not fully-understand the question?

→ How the interviewer reacts to what they're saying. Concentrate on anything where the interviewer seems unimpressed, not happy, or upset. Then see how your competition handled it. Did they notice the reaction? Did they react appropriately and adjust? Did the interviewer's reaction change afterwards?

This is where you can really show what a true business professional you are! When it's your turn to answer or comment, you'll be able to highlight what they said and how they behaved. For example, suppose John and Mary are interviewing along with you. Mary tells the interviewer she has five years experience and no college degree. John mentions he has a college degree but only a year of experience. If you happen to have a college degree and more than a year of experience, you can point that out.

Even better would be to reference Mary and John specifically by name and their information. In other words, let the interviewer know that you're a cross between Mary and John. You have more experience than John, plus a college degree; something Mary happens to lack.

By handling it this way, you're showing how astute you are. You were paying careful attention to everything happening around you. You also showed your ability to make comparisons and differentiate yourself from the crowd. In the workplace, the abilities to focus attention, extrapolate information, make comparisons, and identify similarities and differences are very desirable. You displayed all of these! Now the interviewer will have a very positive impression of you. Some of your competitors may also draw distinctions, but not everyone will reference people by name. Your doing this is an excellent way to standout and impress. It makes you more personable and professional.

Tip #2:   Don't insult anyone or get too cocky

Because your goal is to be the consummate professional, you never want to be rude or insulting. So whenever you refer to what a fellow candidate says, make sure you are always very polite. If you disagree with any of them, clearly state your reason(s) why in a business-like manner. In other words, show an appreciation of their viewpoint, but voice your reasoning as to why you don't agree.

Multiple Applicants and Interviewers

This situation creates the most pressure for many job seekers. The reason is because you not only have more than one candidate in the room with you, but also multiple interviewers asking you questions. To be successful here, you need to sort of combine the techniques from the previous two group interviewing methods.

Before we discuss how to handle this situation, it's important you understand why employers use this interviewing method. One reason is because they may have too many applicants to interview individually. So they decide to lump them together and get through the interviews quicker. And sometimes, you may be interviewing with people applying for other jobs. For example, one interviewer may deal with the managerial positions, while another may handle customer support. Other times, you may be interviewing with other applicants going for the same position as yourself.

Another reason for using this interviewing method is to increase the level of pressure. If you're applying for a position that involves more pressure or is rather hectic, the employer may wish to simulate that situation. Putting you under increased pressure does this. And one last reason for it is to see how you'd behave in a meeting.

For example, if you're applying for a sales job, then it's possible that the employer wants to simulate an environment where you'll be pitching your product or service. It's quite possible that there may be other salespersons in the same room awaiting their turn to present. And there may be a group of people who will decide which salesperson had the best presentation. So it's not uncommon for sales and supervisory applicants to be interviewed in this manner.

The first key to success in this interviewing situation is not to ignore any of the interviewers! I had mentioned this when we focused on your being interviewed alone by multiple interviewers. The same thing applies here. Regardless of whether one interviewer does all the talking, or they alternate, the worst thing you can do is ignore people in that room! So you must periodically look around the room to acknowledge their presence. And once again, you don't want your head constantly swinging from side-to-side. It has to be a natural movement while speaking.

Another thing you want to do is listen very carefully to your competition. Focus on how well they communicate, their backgrounds, and any mistakes you feel they've made. Also look for areas where you differ in a good way. Use that to your advantage by pointing out how you differ. That will make you standout and be recognized! In addition, you don't want to interrupt somebody while they're speaking. That's rude and unprofessional! Wait patiently until your turn to speak comes.

And finally, don't let the increased pressure get to you. Just remember, it's by design. This means you must appear comfortable in order to be successful. Be sure to show the interviewers and your fellow applicants that you know you're the best one and can hold your own! And you aren't feeling overly pressured because you're a true professional. And professionalism dictates being cool under pressure.

Computer-Based Interview

In my opinion, this is the worst interview any job seeker can ever encounter! The reason is because they're conducted entirely by computer. No human interaction is involved at all! There's:

➜ No interviewer listening carefully and reacting to your words, facial expressions, and body language
➜ No opportunity to clarify or explain things in more detail
➜ Nobody to ask if a question is confusing or unclear
➜ No way you can ask the interviewer questions

In other words, you are entirely on your own! Most often, computer-based interviews are used for the same purpose as phone interviews—to screen applicants. Job hunters typically encounter these interviews when dealing with larger companies. That's because they tend to receive a larger number of applications on a regular basis. With limited staff and time, computers can be more effective in handling the increased volume.

For example, I once applied to a major retailer in my area for some part-time work. The application process consisted of my sitting in front of a computer screen and entering all my information into an online application. After completing this step, it was time for my interview. The computer asked me a series of questions and I selected my answers from the various choices. When I finished the last one, my interview was over.

How can you improve your chances of success? By understanding computers are totally incapable of making judgments. This means it looks at your answers as being either right or wrong. In other words, there's *no* room for interpretation. So when approaching each question, ask yourself what the *best* answer would be out of all the given choices!

You must realize the vast majority of computer-based interviews consist of multiple-choice and/or true-false questions. This make it easier for the machine to grade and levels the playing field. That's because every applicant is given the exact same choices. If you don't agree with any of the given choices, you must still choose the *best* one out of them. With fill-in-the-blank, short answer, or essay questions, it's much harder for a machine to score. For example, a candidate may misspell something or use different wording.

Quite often, you're presented with questions that test your personality, decision-making, and integrity. You must look good and do the right thing! You'll also tend to get scenarios to test how you might handle yourself on the job. These are the ones where you'll often see choices you disagree with. In other words, how you'd handle it won't be among the choices. Now since you cannot add choices or type explanations, you must select the *best* answer.

Hands-on or Project Interview

This method of interviewing is an excellent way to really test a candidate's ability to handle the job. It involves the interviewer giving you actual hands-on practice doing a particular task or group of tasks.

For instance, with teaching positions, it's very common to be given something known as a *test-teach* as part of the hiring process. That involves your actually conducting (teaching) a class. Generally, you'll have 10-20 minutes to instruct students on a particular subject. Sometimes, you are given a topic to teach; other times, it's left up to you.

The whole purpose here is to actually see you in action! It's also to get a real feel for how instruct and handle yourself in the classroom. Your students will most often be other faculty, staff, and/or management personnel. And you're teaching style, instructional methods, classroom management, ability to answer questions, etc are all being evaluated.

Another example is your being given a project to take home and work on. You'll be given a specific deadline as to when it needs to be completed and turned-in. And you're being tested on your ability to meet deadlines, follow instructions, and do quality work. In addition, you're professionalism and knowledge are also being evaluated.

Tip #1:   Be prepared for an early deadline

It's quite common to be given an unrealistic deadline just to increase the level of stress and pressure. That's to see how well you can handle yourself and to simulate a real world scenario. In fact, many job hunters are caught totally by surprise at being given a project or an unrealistic deadline and don't know how to react.

Remember, anything can and often does happen in an interview. So I strongly suggest you expect the unexpected. And just remain calm and do your best within the given timeframe. If you really are knowledgeable and perhaps experienced, then you should be able to handle it well-enough to get through it. And that's what they're looking for.

Tip #2:   Follow all instructions very carefully

As a professional, you should be able to follow instructions. So read and listen to everything very carefully! For example, if they want a coversheet on blue paper, then make sure you do it. Or if margins are to be set a certain way, you want to make sure your are formatted properly.

Tip #3:   Do your best

This should be a given, but I'll say it anyway. Regardless of whether or not you feel you were given enough time to complete the project, it's critical to success that you put your best efforts into it! Why? Because that's the most anybody can do. And it's exactly what an employer expects from you. True, you may not have done as well as you would have if you had more time, but your ability to handle yourself well under pressure and deadlines is what's being tested here. So you have to do "well-enough" in the employer's mind to get through.

PART 3:

Interview Question Types

There are many different types of questions that you could encounter in your job search. Each one is designed to gather information from you in a different way. This section will discuss what they are so you'll be prepared for them. I strongly suggest you not skip over this section!

Open and Closed-End

These are the most commonly asked type of questions in nearly every interview. So you should definitely be ready for them. A *closed-end* question, sometimes called a *directive*, is basically a yes and no or true-false type question. It's designed to get a short and very precise response from the applicant.

For example: *Do you speak a foreign language?* Notice how I'm not asking you which language(s) you speak, but rather if you speak any. So your answer is a simple yes or no. Another example would be: *How many years experience do you have in human resources?* Once again, all I'm asking for is a very short and sweet answer, such as 2 years. I'm not asking for details about your experience, but rather the amount of experience you have.

Closed-end questions are also used to test one's knowledge or expertise. For instance: *What does CPU stand for?* Here, I'm testing your knowledge of computer terminology. CPU stands for central processing unit. Once again, a very short and precise answer. And there's often a right and a wrong answer. So it can be used as a quick honesty checker!

You'll encounter many of these questions with phone interviews because they're relatively short. And these questions can be a good way to get very specific answers in a short amount of time. It's also a good way to get a lot of questions asked in a short timeframe. They're also common in computer-based interviews for the same reason. But that doesn't mean other interviewing methods won't use them too; they will. So be prepared for them regardless of your interview's format.

By contrast, *open-ended* or *non-directive* questions are designed to get a more broader answer. In other words, they're not simply yes and no type questions. They require the applicant give a longer and more detailed answer.

For example: *What do you know about our company?* This isn't a question that can simply be answered with a yes or a no. Instead, it requires you to talk more and go into some detail in your answer. So it's designed to get you to speak more and provide the interviewer with additional information.

Situational and Problem-Solving

These two are more complex than closed or open-ended questions. And their purpose is slightly different. *Situational* questions are designed to get information about your insight, judgment, and knowledge. They ask you what-if scenarios to see how you'd handle various situations.

For example: *What would you do if you had to work late?* This question is one where every candidate could have an individual response. In other words, it's possible that no two will respond the same way. It's wide-open!

A *problem-solving* question expands upon the situational. It's designed to probe more deeply into your thinking and ability to handle things. For example: *You're working on the budget and the numbers don't seem to add-up. How would you fix this?* This requires you to do some thinking and resolve an issue. Once again, each candidate could have a different response or approach. But it's looking at how competent you are in dealing with potentially real situations on the job!

These types of questions are becoming much more common today. So I definitely suggest preparing yourself for them! And majority of them are centered on actual situations you may encounter on the job. In others, they give you a sense of what the actual job may be like. So they benefit you as well as the interviewer! And the interviewer will be focusing on your approach and analysis of the situation.

Behavioral and Follow-up

Behavioral questions are designed to see how well you've handled a particular situation before. For example: *Tell me about a time when you had to deal with a difficult customer.* Here, I'm asking you to tell me about a specific situation and how you handled it. This will give me an excellent sense of how you'd perform on the job! And how you might handle a similar situation if it came up again. Once again, individual responses and approaches could vary. But it's concentrating on how well you've handled yourself before.

Follow-up questions are designed to probe more deeply or to clarify something that has been said. For example, if you answered my question, but that raised something else, I could ask a follow-up. The important thing here is that could be asked at any point! And after your response to any other type of question! So be prepared for follow-up questions after every response. That way, you're ready just in case.

PART 4:

Common Interview Questions

This section is the biggest and our main focus. We'll be discussing a variety of commonly asked questions that you may encounter during an interview.

Tell Me About Yourself

I would have to say that most, if not all books on interviewing, have this extremely important and common question in it. Many of them even give you a number of responses you can use. But the one thing I've noticed is they seem to miss the main point, which is "Why are you even being asked this question in the very first place?"

Here's the ultimate key to interview success! Knowing the purpose behind each and every single question you are asked. Now that's much easier said than done. But with my help, you'll be more prepared and can greatly improve your chances.

So what is the purpose behind the question "Tell me about yourself?" Does the interviewer really want to hear about your skills? Your experience? Your education? Well it might surprise you to learn the answer is actually no. Then what exactly does the interviewer want?

What the interviewer is really doing here is testing you. But as you'll soon discover, each and every single interview question asked has a very specific purpose behind it. In other words, there's always something on which a potential new hire is being tested. The most successful interview is one where the applicant has correctly identified what that test is. Here is where *Think Like an Interviewer* comes in handy. I'll help you discover what the interviewer is actually testing with certain questions. Helping you to mold your answers and increase your chances for success.

So getting back to the question "Tell me about yourself," let's now see what the real purpose behind this question is. With this particular question, the interviewer is testing your ability to organize and communicate your thoughts. The interviewer wants to see how well you speak, organize, and communicate your thoughts.

   KEY #1:　　What you say isn't as important as how well you say it!

Whatever you say, your words and sentences must be arranged logically. You must also speak extremely well, with one sentence flowing nicely into the next.

Here are some helpful tips:

➔ Although the interviewer's main focus in on how well you speak, I feel it's best to limit what you say.

I've known candidates who've spoken about their hobbies and other unrelated things. As long as you speak well, you're showing the interviewer excellent communication skills. That's exactly what the interviewer wants. But I feel it's best you limit yourself to talking about your qualifications, experience, and desire to work for the company. Doing this emphasizes the fact you're a good speaker and are business-oriented. Remember, you're being interviewed for job where you'll be paid to work, not have fun. So I feel that focusing more on your business-side emphasizes your understanding of this and makes you look better.

Now some people just begin talking about their background and qualifications, which is perfectly fine. Others will ask the interviewer which area(s) should be the main focus of their responses. This way, your answer is more tailored around what the interviewer wants. Both approaches work well and are personal choices. I've used them both and have gotten positive results.

➔ Make sure you're always speaking at a good rate of speed

In other words, don't talk too fast nor too slow. For example, my having moved from the Northeast to the Northwest meant slowing down my rate of speech. That's because people in the Northeast tend to speak faster than those in the Northwest or in the South. My point is you want the interviewer to be able to easily hear what you have to say. Talking too fast makes the words fly by so quickly that important things can easily get missed. Talking too slow can make an interview rather tedious and boring.

Just imaging speaking to a customer in a very slow voice and basically putting that customer to sleep. Does this project a positive image of your company? No! That's exactly why you always want to make a positive impression. You accomplish this by making sure you speak in a manner that isn't too fast nor too slow, but just right. It's hard to say exactly how fast this is. But it needs to be a pace where your words are easily understood and you won't put someone to sleep.

➔ Use an appropriate level of volume so the interviewer can easily hear your every word

In other words, don't talk too loud nor too soft. A loud or booming voice will make an interviewer say, "Tone it down." Too soft a voice will cause an interviewer to say, "Speak-up." Either way, you won't look good. And since this question is usually asked at the very beginning of an interview, you didn't get off to a very good start. This can severely hurt your chances. Just remember the old saying, "First impressions are lasting ones." You must always make a good first impression!

➔ Always speak in a clear and concise manner without being overly wordy.

In other words, keep it short, sweet, and to the point. Your purpose here is to present an overview and not every single detail! You want to grab the interviewer's attention so he or she is impressed and wants to know more.

➔ Stay on-point at all times!

Bouncing around is a clear sign of poor organization, which makes you look very bad. You want to show you are well-organized and capable of logical thought. Now for those of you who've taken some interviews already, you may have run into an interviewer who looks away while you're speaking. Or had one staring endlessly at your resume. Let me tell you that these behaviors are not at all uncommon and here's why. The interviewer is actually focusing very intently on your every word. He or she just doesn't want to be distracted by other things, like your body language and facial expressions. An interviewer will sometimes do lots of writing just to throw a candidate off his or her game. But in reality, the interviewer is paying very close attention to exactly how you're speaking. Every step of the way, judging your ability to effectively communicate.

KEY #2:   Don't be phased by any of this and/or lower your voice

These are both very common reactions when somebody doesn't appear to be paying attention. Instead, you should handle things in one of two ways. Deciding which one to use is strictly a matter of personal choice because they both work equally well. Some of you may feel more comfortable using one method. Others may want to vary their approaches to add some variety or see if one works a little better.

Method #1:   Keep on speaking as though nothing is wrong

Doing this shows you're fully-aware of the question's main purpose to simply test your communication skills. Because what you say isn't as important as how you say it, there's really no need to stop.

Method #2:   Stop and ask the interviewer if you should focus on something else in particular

For example, you could ask if you should discuss your education or your work experience, etc. This way, you're asking the interviewer for some guidance in terms of what should be addressed in your response. Handling the question in this way makes you look like a true professional. This is because you come across as someone who doesn't want to waste anybody's time talking about unimportant or irrelevant things. Instead, you want to zero right in on the main point. This is a very business-like thing to do and illustrates the notion of time is money. It also shows you don't want to waste the interviewer's time.

But as I said earlier, which of these two methods you ultimately decide to use is strictly up to you. I've used them both and found them equally effective. In either case, the most important thing to remember is to speak well and in a logical manner!

The bottom-line is:

1. The question "Tell me about yourself" most often forms the interviewer's first impression of you. An impression that can last throughout your entire interview. So you must begin on a very high note.
2. Don't memorize exactly what you're going to say! I've seen plenty of people do this over the years. Most do it so they won't mess-up during their interviews, which is perfectly understandable. But the problem is you'll tend to sound scripted or rehearsed.
3. You're interviewing for a job and not a television show or play. This means you must sound like yourself and not a robot. In other words, you need to sound more natural. So you must demonstrate the ability to think on your feet.
4. Have some idea in advance what you'd like to focus on, or ask the interviewer directly what he or she would like you to address. This way, your words will flow more naturally.
5. Never speak right away! This is a classic interview mistake because it shows you don't think before taking action. An interviewer must see you took some time to organize things and choose your words carefully.

6. Just think of all the people who've put their foot in their mouth because they spoke too soon or said the wrong thing. Always remember that first impressions are lasting ones! You are being judged on how good of an impression you make. A poor one will hurt and be remembered. But a good one will help and impress.

7. Take a brief moment to think so you can decide what you want to say and how to organize it.

8. Remember that success in business lies in thinking ahead. That's part of what's being tested. So don't rush in and possibly make mistakes. Consider what to say and how to organize your thoughts first. This demonstrates solid planning and organization.

9. But don't take too long! If you do, the interviewer may begin to feel that you are unable to think on your feet. That can hurt your chances.

10. Always speak with confidence and pride. Confidence in your own abilities and desire to work there. Pride in your accomplishments and doing a good job. But don't go overboard with your confidence to the point where you seem arrogant. Your goal is to show you believe in yourself.

11. Speak clearly by making sure you're not too loud, too soft, too fast, nor too slow.

12. Avoid speaking in a monotone voice by varying your pitch (tone of voice) from time-to-time. This will help you hold the interviewer's attention and prevent things from becoming rather boring.

13. Pay very close attention to the interviewer's reaction to your words as you're speaking. You do this to gauge how well it's being received. I suggest focusing your attention on the interviewer's facial expressions and body language as strong indicators.

14. For example, if you get the sense an interviewer doesn't seem to like what he or she is hearing at that moment, then be sure you adjust accordingly.

15. When an interviewer doesn't like what he or she is hearing, your failure to pick-up on this and change course will only make matters worse. **FYI**: This is one of the hardest things to master!

Tip: Go look at yourself in a mirror and pretend. Pretend you heard something you like and see how you react. Do the same for something you didn't like. This can help you pick-up on these subtle things more easily because people tend to react in similar fashions.

16. Whatever you say in your response, be sure to end with briefly explaining why you feel this job is for you. Also mention why you believe you'll do a good job if hired. That's because people tend to remember the last thing they hear.

17. You're letting the interviewer know right from the start that you believe you are a good match for this position. This makes you look good right from the start and tells the interviewer you've thought about how you'd fit-in. Besides, not everyone will do this and so you've separated yourself out from the crowd in a good way!

Strengths and Weaknesses

Some interviewers word this as a single question. In other words, they'll ask you about both together. Others will divide it into two separate questions. One will center on your strengths; the other will concentrate on your weaknesses. There are also plenty of variations to this question. Here are a few examples:

➔ What would you say your strengths are?
➔ If I asked you what your weaknesses were, what would you say?
➔ What do you consider your greatest strength to be?
➔ What would you say is your biggest weakness?

But regardless of how the question is actually worded, does the interviewer really want to know about your strengths and/or weaknesses? The answer to this is both yes and no.

Yes, the interviewer is somewhat interested in the ones you list. But what's really being tested here is your ability to do an honest self-evaluation or assessment of yourself. In other words, it's a test of how well you know yourself and whether or not you'll level with me—the interviewer.

You're also being tested on your problem-solving ability when it comes to your weaknesses. This is something many job seekers fail to recognize! It's also a big reason why many hate this question or mishandle it.

Most of us don't have a problem talking about our strengths because we usually know the things we're good at. We're also proud to discuss them because they're good things. But when it comes to discussing our weaknesses, we're either:

➔ Too afraid to say what they are out of fear we'll look bad
➔ Unsure what they are or just can't think of anything
➔ Devoid of any weaknesses, or at least none worth mentioning

Now some experts advise taking a strength and turning it into a weakness. For example: *People have told me I'm too punctual.* You're taking *punctuality*, which is a good thing, and are turning it into a weakness by saying you having too much of it. Well let me tell you that an experienced interviewer can spot this BS a mile a way!

Other experts suggest mentioning an actual, yet small weakness. The majority also suggest picking a weakness that's unrelated to the job. This is so you won't make yourself look bad in front of the interviewer. Revealing a bigger and job-related weakness might do this.

But I disagree with these approaches and here's why. The interviewer is more interested in your handling of the weakness than the actual weakness itself. An interviewer wants some reassurance your weakness won't hinder or prevent you from doing well on the job. Your identifying and taking action to eliminate the weakness offers this reassurance. It sends the message that you have everything under control. So it's not going to impact your ability to do the job and hurt you.

KEY: Identify a real weakness and show how you've dealt, are dealing, or intend to deal with it

Using my approach, you'll come across as someone who's both honest and a good problem-solver. You were honest enough to reveal an actual weakness. Then you found an *effective* way to improve. In other words, your decision to take action got positive results.

When the interviewer pictures you on the job, he or she will see your making an honest assessment of the situation. And you'll be seen coming-up with workable solutions. These are qualities crucial to success in the workplace!

Perfect example, I've always been a poor speller, which many job seekers would be deftly afraid of telling an interviewer. Especially for clerical positions where you may have to: write letters and e-mails, do some data entry, prepare contracts and proposals, etc. But I've never been afraid to mention my poor spelling during an interview. The reason is because I've worked on improving my spelling and it's gotten better. Now I make fewer mistakes.

The point is that I've:

1.   Successfully identified a problem—poor spelling
2.   Taken appropriate corrective action—exercises, etc
3.   Achieved positive results—fewer mistakes

What I've done here is show an interviewer the desirable qualities of:

→ Honesty and truthfulness
→ Willingness to deal with a problem
→ Wise decision-making
→ Effective problem-solving
→ Positive results, meaning improvement

Everything here is something an interviewer will respect and admire, so I look more impressive. What I've effectively done is taken what would ordinarily be viewed as a negative, and turned it into something that will now be perceived more positively. How? By showing an ability to identify and deal with a problem. This is exactly what an interviewer needs to see from you!

Tip #1:   Don't hint or say you have no weaknesses

This is a huge mistake because nobody's perfect! So telling an interviewer you lack even the slightest little weakness is very arrogant and cocky of you. Doing this will severely hurt your chances of achieving success.

Tip #2:   Have someone else tell you what your strengths and weaknesses are, including your biggest ones.

I suggest this because many people have a tough time seeing their own strengths and weaknesses. Getting someone else's perspective can be extremely helpful. Perhaps they'll see something you don't or view things differently. This can give you an excellent indication as to how an interviewer might actually perceive you. Just make sure you ask someone who knows you well.

Tip #3:   If that person tells you something you don't like nor agree with, don't get upset

Your goal is to see how you come across to others so you can project a very positive image of yourself during an interview. Getting an honest assessment from an outsider can definitely help you identify your strengths. It can also point-out areas in need of improvement. So approach things from this perspective.

The bottom-line is:

1.   Be completely honest and open.
2.   When talking about your strengths, speak with pride and confidence. But don't cross over into the realm of arrogance and cockiness. In other words, speak proudly! After all, you're talking about something good.
3.   Your facial expressions and body language should also project the image of being proud when talking about your strengths. So smile, speak-up, and appear confident.
4.   Do the same thing when discussing how you've overcome your weaknesses. In other words, be proud of your decision to deal with your problem and resolve it.

Tip #4:   Most interviewers are skilled in reading one's body language and facial expression. That means they may pick-up on differences between your words and body language. So be sure you match them up! This way, you'll appear more believable.

5.   When asked about your strengths, don't mention ones that aren't related in some way to the workplace. Your answer should center on the qualities that can and do lead to success.
6.   When discussing your weaknesses, be sure to explain how you plan on handling or have actually handled it. This will focus the interviewer's attention on your strong problem-solving and decision-making abilities.
7.   In other words, identify a problem, devise a workable solution, put that solution into action, and measure the effectiveness of your decision. Lastly, show the interviewer you made smart decisions by displaying confidence in them.
8.   Don't let the volume level of your voice drop too low, which is a pretty common mistake when talking about your weaknesses.
9.   It almost seems as though it's human nature not to want to talk about the bad. So we often lower our voices to de-emphasize it. But during an interview, you want to keep your voice at an appropriate volume level to show you're not afraid. It's also to emphasize the point that you've successfully identified a problem and have come-up with an appropriate solution.

Where You See Yourself in the Future

This can be phrased in a number of different ways. For example:

→ Where do you see yourself in 3 to 5 years?
→ Where do you think you'll be in 10 years?
→ Where do you think you'll be in the future?
→ Where do you see yourself in the near future?

Regardless of how the question is actually worded, it seems perfectly straightforward. The interviewer obviously wants to know your aspirations down the road, correct? Well the answer is both yes and no. The real key here is that you're being tested on your ability to set goals and develop an effective plan to reach them. It's also a test of your decision-making ability because you're making choices and facing the consequences of those choices.

In the workplace, planning and achieving goals are vital to a company's success. It doesn't matter what company it is nor what they do. All companies have goals and strategies. So an interviewer is really determining whether or not a potential new hire has these same abilities. If not, then problems could be looming in the distance. Problems caused by a failure to plan ahead, set goals, and adjust along the way. In other words, failing to plan ahead is just a recipe for disaster.

Fact is, we make decisions all the time whether it's for personal or business reasons. In our own personal lives, we make decisions such as:

→ What to wear today
→ What to eat for dinner
→ What to watch on television
→ When it's time to go to bed
→ How to spend, save, and invest our money
→ Where to take a vacation, what sites to see, and at what hotel we should stay

Some decisions made in the workplace include:

→ How our day should be arranged or organized
→ What we should be working on right now
→ Which customers to follow-up on, call, or visit
→ Deciding what shifts or hours people should work next week or month
→ By how much should we increase or lower our prices
→ Which new products we should carry and sell

➔ Who's employee review or evaluation should we do next

The point I'm making is that planning, goal-setting, risk-management, and decision-making all tend to go together. This is exactly what an interviewer is testing with the question of where you see yourself down the road. In other words, do you have these abilities within you? If so, are you any good at them? To be successful here, the interviewer must see that the answer to *both* parts is yes!

So how should you handle these questions? By showing the interviewer you've given careful thought to both your career and your future. In other words, an interviewer really wants to see that you've set clear and realistic (practical) short and long-term goals for yourself. But more importantly, that you have a plan of action to reach them!

Benchmarks are a way to measure your progress and to see how well things are going. They help to keep you on-track so you can achieve your goals. They're also used to assess whether or not any adjustments need to be made for whatever reason(s). An interviewer wants a clear sense that you've:

1. Put a great deal of thought into your career plans
2. Assessed the potential risks involved or barriers you could face
3. Developed a sensible plan to achieve your objective(s).

The interviewer also wants to see how his or her company and position fit into your plans. If the interviewer gets the sense you're only there for the money or something unrelated to your career objective(s), then you won't look good at all. But you'll look very good if the interviewer can see that you've:

➔ Put a lot of thought into it
➔ Set realistic and achievable goals
➔ Explained exactly how *this* company and job fit right in

The bottom-line is:

1. Have realistic short and long-term goals that could be achieved. In other words, be practical and show that you have a plan to get to where you want.
2. Understand that in business, short-term generally means 1 to 3 years into the future. Long-term tends to mean 5 years and beyond. Part of what an interviewer is testing is whether or not you realize this. So I suggest having both short and long-term career goals in mind ahead of time. That way, you're full-prepared for however they word their question.
3. Have a suitable plan with appropriate benchmarks along the way to measure and evaluate your progress. This tells an interviewer that you understand the goal-setting process and know it's important to have a standard for measuring and evaluating your progress.
4. Clearly explain how the interviewer's company fits-in with your career objective(s).
5. Display confidence in your decisions along the way, and in your hopes of achieving your goals. If you don't appear confident that you'll ultimately get there, then you're either second-guessing yourself and/or know failure is ahead. Showing either or both of these during an interview simply makes you look bad. Always remember that interviewers picture you on the job. So you must project yourself in a positive light at all times!

Why Hire You?

The question of why an employer should hire you over other applicants is a really great question in my opinion. But it's also one many candidates have a pretty tough time answering. The reason is because their backgrounds are quite often very similar to those of other candidates. So they just don't know how to separate themselves out from those others.

But the key word in this question is you. What the interviewer is testing here is your ability to standout and differentiate yourself from the crowd by getting you to say, "You really want to hire *me* because …" You are also being tested on your ability to comprehend what it takes to do well in this job. And what it takes to be successful in this profession.

Now a very common mistake is to become too cocky or arrogant by saying something along the lines of "I'm the best!" What's wrong with this? It makes you look bad because you're putting others down and are taking a pretty high and mighty attitude. In other words, an interviewer will see you as having a swelled head who lauds it over all others. This makes it appear as though you're better than everyone else. Confidence is always good, but a swelled or overly-inflated sense of importance is not.

KEY #1:   Know your competition very well

KEY #2:   Clearly explain what makes you different from all the others

KEY #3:   Know what type of person and background are needed to be successful in both this job and field

But will you really know the names of others applying for this job? Perhaps, but most likely, the answer is no. The most important thing to realize here is not knowing their names, but rather the backgrounds you think they'll have. It's a test to see if you really know what skills, experience, education, personality, etc it takes to do well in this job and/or profession.

For example, if I'm applying for a job in customer service, then I should already know it requires someone who's a good communicator and problem-solver. Someone with patience and understanding who can relate well to others and get things done. So it's a pretty good bet that many, if not most of the other applicants, will possess these same qualities. The issue now becomes, "What more do I offer that they may not?"

The interviewer is trying to discover whether you have a clear understanding of the qualities necessary for someone to do well in this job or profession. If so, what do *you* have that would make an interviewer stand up and say, "I want to hire this person!" This is where you need to take a good hard look at yourself and self-evaluate your qualities and abilities.

For instance, perhaps you:

➜ Feel you're more experienced in the job than others
➜ Think you have a level of education or some training others might lack
➜ Have experience working at different types of companies when others may have concentrated in just one
➜ Approach or see things in a unique or unusual way

In other words, each of us has a special quality that makes us standout from others. An interviewer wants to know what yours is.

Tip #1: Take a piece of paper and draw a line down the middle. On one side, put the amount of experience and education you have. On the other, put what you think your average competitor might have. Now do the same thing for your individual skills, talents, and any other specific things you've done that could be relevant to the job you're seeking. Carefully look at this when you're done to see how you compare. Highlight areas where you think you exceed your competition.

During your interview, mention those areas where you believe you exceed other candidates. You're not only showcasing your solid researching ability, but also demonstrating the abilities to make and draw distinctions.

Tip #2: Take a good look at the way you approach various tasks and situations. Look for differences in how your approach might differ from others.

If so, then mention it to show an interviewer how you standout and differ. In other words, explain the difference(s) in how you operate and approach things. If you feel your approach is better, then you can explain your reason(s) why. But be very careful in saying or implying others are wrong! It's all right to point-out differences or areas where you may disagree. But avoid any hint of being viewed as insulting or calling somebody else stupid or incompetent. You want to be seen as the consummate professional

Tip #3: Look at multiple job descriptions and requirements in various places. See what's required and what's preferred or desired.

The reason why I suggest this is because it can help you show an employer what they'd be getting if they were to hire you. You'll be in a much better position to show them how you measure-up and compare in terms of what they'd like. And it gives you a sense of what your competition may have.

Required means the employer considers it to be absolutely necessary to performing and succeeding on the job. It's an employer's way of telling you a candidate *must*, at the very least, have it. These are the minimum requirements all applicants must possess. So assume the majority of your competition will have these same skills, abilities, and qualities!

Preferred or *desired* means it isn't required, but would be a nice thing to have in a candidate. Here is where employers have tremendous flexibility in choosing among candidates. For example, one applicant may have just one of these desired skills. Another may have two or three. Who do you think is more likely to get the job? The one with those two or three additional skills. So I suggest concentrating most of your efforts in this area.

Tip #4:   For those of you seeking employment in graphic or web design, I suggest taking a good look at other websites and graphics.

This way, you not only can offer your opinion(s), but also some idea(s) of your own. If you feel you could improve upon things, then explain how. This allows you to show them exactly what you're capable of doing. It also provides a good incentive for them to hire you. Maybe you can even offer some advice to help improve their own website or graphics.

The bottom-line is:

1. Demonstrate your understanding of what it takes to achieve success in both this job and profession. In other words, the qualities, training, skills, backgrounds, etc that would be needed.
2. Show a good sense of who your competition might be.

Tip #5:   Going to job fairs and listening to others as they speak with employers is a great way to gauge your competition. Maybe you'll be able to sneak-a-peek at their resumes or talk directly to some of your competitors.

3. Do an honest self-evaluation of yourself to discover what makes you standout from the crowd in a good way. Then be proud to say it!
4. But don't toot your own horn too much or you'll be perceived as being rather arrogant and cocky. Remember, this isn't television; this is real life! So you must always project the image of a true professional.
5. Be sure to explain why you think you'll fit-in nicely with this company and it's personnel. You do this by showing how your talents will compliment and ultimately benefit them. In other words, an interview is where you sell yourself to an employer without being too high and mighty.
6. It's *essential* you show how you'd prove to be a valuable addition and compliment them, if only you were given the chance. In other words, take the attitude of "I can make a real and positive contribution to your company if given the opportunity. That means both of us will benefit in the end. Now you're saying you're a worthwhile investment!

Tip #6:   If you have samples of your best or high quality work, bring them with you to the interview! Now you'll have something concrete an interviewer can look at that shows firsthand what you're capable of doing.

7. Make sure anything confidential is crossed-out before showing or giving it to an interviewer. Information such as: account, social security, or credit card numbers. Also be sure it's crossed-out dark enough so the interviewer won't be able to read through it.
8. Using a black marker and then photocopying it tends to work well here. I also suggest bringing copies for the interviewer to keep and put in the files. This way, he or she will have something to refer back to if needed. It also spotlights your abilities to plan ahead and protect confidential information.

Ideal Job

The key word here is "ideal," meaning dream or perfect. In the real world, we most often have to settle for something that's less than perfect or ideal. With this question, the interviewer is testing your personality to see what kind of person you really are.

Your own sense of what you consider to be the perfect job tells me—the interviewer—a great deal about you as a person. That's exactly what the interviewer wants to evaluate and judge. For example, if your ideal job is one where you are simply paid extremely well and do little, that tells me you want it easy, meaning you're lazy. This certainly doesn't make you look good at all.

An interviewer is really gauging your overall personality and dreams by looking at things like:

- → How far from reality your dream job is
- → Whether it's completely unrelated to the kind of work or career you're seeking
- → If you want the good life handed to you
- → If you even want to work at all
- → Whether you're a more high or low pressure individual

So how do you handle the question about your dream or ideal job? Well you should present an honest sense of who you are as a person. You want to show you're willing to work hard to get to where you want to be. Not simply have things handed to you on a silver platter. You also want the interviewer to see you are fully-aware life isn't always fair. And understand everything doesn't always turn out the way you want or hope it'll be. Nor is life ideal. It's also important to show this is all right with you because you honestly believe you'll ultimately get to where you want to be. And you'll happy in the end.

The bottom-line is:

1. Have an ideal job or work environment in mind prior to your interview.
2. Don't be overly idealistic nor appear as though you're completely out of touch with reality. It's perfectly fine to have hopes and dreams beyond reality. But straying too far won't make you look good if the interviewer begins to feel there's no way you'll ever find this.
3. I suggest making your ideal something more positive in nature where you'll show a good work ethic. Not something way out in left field, meaning completely out of touch with the world.
4. Explain that you know the world isn't always fair. Nor is the world ideal. But you do have a clear sense of what you want and where you want to be down the road.
5. Show how *this* job somehow fits-in with your ideal one. In other words, make the connection that although this job may not be the ideal, it's definitely something you'll enjoy. That way, the interviewer understands you're being realistic, have thought things through, and are here because you want to be.
6. Explain that you honestly feel you can handle this job. All you're looking for is the chance or opportunity to prove yourself. If given that chance, you'll show them what a smart decision it was to hire you.

Knowledge About Our Company

This is a frequently asked question and rightly so in my professional opinion. Why? Because it's a good test of your ability to gather information and do research. These are very important skills in the workplace.

Having employees who are capable of doing them, even on their most basic level, is a desirable quality. But it might surprise you how many applicants are caught off-guard with this question or try to BS their way through it. You see, the inherent attitude of an interviewer is this:

→ If you were smart, you'd take the time to do some basic research and learn something about us. Even if it was just who we are and what we do.

Therefore, you must be prepared and ready! So what does basic research mean? It includes gathering information such as:

1. What the company actually does—their main business
2. How long they've been in business
3. The products and/or services they provide
4. Locations or major markets in which they operate

But in my professional opinion, it's always best to go that "extra mile" and do more than just basic research. In other words, do some more "advanced" research and read-up on a company to learn as much as you can. Why do I make this suggestion? Because this is where you can really highlight your researching capabilities and standout from your competition!

For example, you can:

→ Take a look at their annual corporate report. This can be an *invaluable* resource because it's usually full of bullet points highlighting their activities and performance. Even if you can't read it all, just skimming the front section can give you lots of great information!
→ Visit their website
→ Watch and/or listen to the business station(s)
→ Keep up with current news and events

In other words, focus the interviewer's attention on the fact you not only always try your best to gather current and updated information, but also know where to look. Fact is, not everyone listens to, reads, or watches the news. Nor would they take the time to see if there was some recent news about this company or the industry.

But your doing this tells an interviewer you're willing to go above and beyond, and are fully capable of gathering relevant information. It showcases your ability to gather and relay information, and can definitely separate you out from your competition!

The bottom-line is:

1. At the very least, know some basic facts about the company to which you're interviewing or the industry in which they operate.
2. Be completely open to learning more about them and seek it out whenever and wherever possible.

Tip: Picking-up a company brochure or visiting them ahead of time to scope them out are both great ways to demonstrate your solid researching skills.

3. Visit the company's website and check out some of their links. Important ones include the pages talking about the company itself (overview or details), news events and press releases, products and services offered, listing of departments, and important or key personnel.
4. Watch or listen to the news, *both* local and network! Quite often, people tend to focus on just one or the other. But looking at both will give you further insight.
5. Look for anything you feel is related in some way. In other words, it doesn't even have to be news about this particular company. It just needs to be something you feel would be important to them. For example, a recent news item on a competitor still shows good research and is something that may interest the interviewer.
6. Demonstrate your solid communication, logical thought, and strategic thinking by briefly explaining to the interviewer how you feel this relates to them. In other words, connect the dots. Remember, when you show desirable traits and qualities, you're looking good!
7. Look for any advertising specials the company is currently offering or has recently offered. Check the newspapers, listen to the radio, watch television, look for flyers, etc. This not only shows your ability to conduct research, but also shows a personal knowledge of what's going with them. Now believe me when I say this will really impress an interviewer!

Handling Pressure

The question of how you handle pressure can be worded in a number of ways. For instance, the interviewer may ask you:

- → How would you describe or rate your ability to handle pressure?
- → Which do you prefer, a more or less pressured work environment?
- → How do you deal with pressure?
- → Do you work well under pressure?
- → Do you like pressure?
- → Would you say that you thrive under pressure?

But regardless of how this particular question is worded, the point is an interviewer is essentially testing your personality. The interviewer wants to see if you are the type of person who enjoys or thrives under pressure. But that isn't the only thing being tested. You're also being tested on how well you behave and perform under pressure. Lastly, the interviewer is testing some researching skills by seeing if you even know whether or not this job or profession tends to be more or less pressured.

Now the key to handling the question about pressure is to be able to demonstrate you can do a good job in both settings. Even if you don't particularly like pressure, the simple fact is that work can sometimes becomes more pressured. Here are just a few examples of how pressure can increase:

- → Everything is moved-up because a deadline has suddenly changed
- → A policy change has increased your paperwork or workload
- → You need to cover for a co-worker who has resigned or been terminated So your workload has basically doubled
- → There was a management change and you aren't sure if you'll like or get along with the new boss
- → Your boss is in a bad mood and is taking it out on you
- → A nasty customer is yelling and screaming at you
- → Business was slow and you didn't make as much Now you have to work even harder next month
- → You didn't get the promotion or raise you wanted Or somebody else got it instead of you

Sometimes these kind of things happen with plenty of advanced warning. Other times, they happen with little warning. But in many cases, they just happen without any warning at all. My point is that some degree of pressure is just a normal part of working life. An interviewer is testing to see if you are aware of this.

But an interviewer is also getting a firsthand look at how well you can deal with some actual pressure. Just being interviewed puts a candidate under real pressure. You're under pressure to:

➔ Say the right thing by giving appropriate answers to my unannounced, and perhaps totally unexpected questions
➔ Make and maintain a good impression at all times
➔ Control your body movements and language at all times For example, not shaking or moving around too much, rambling on, or stumbling in some fashion
➔ Get through the interview and make it to the next round—a second interview, additional testing, etc

My point is that pressure is just a given. Some people thrive and enjoy it; others do not. But it's very important to realize the personalities are quite different between those who like or enjoy pressure, and those who do not. Interviewers know this and are trying to determine which category you fit into. To be successful, you must show that no matter which category you fall into, you can still perform your task(s) well.

The bottom-line is:

1. Be mindful of the potential work environment. Know whether this profession tends to be a more or a less-pressured one. For example, commission sales tends to be more high-pressured.
2. Tell the interviewer which type of work environment you prefer (more or less pressure), but don't stop there!
3. Continue on to explain that you can do well in both. This way, the interviewer can see you'll be successful regardless of the environment in which you'll actually be working.
4. Giving an interviewer specific examples of how well you've handled pressure before always work best! That's because it's not just your own opinion or feeling, but rather something concrete you've actually done. It's the philosophy of "If you've done it before, then you can do it again."
5. Appear relaxed at all times to demonstrate firsthand your actual performance under pressure. As I said earlier, an interview by its very nature puts a candidate under some pressure. This is where you *must* show how well you can handle it.
6. To an interviewer, if an applicant can't even handle the light pressures of an interview, then he or she most certainly can't deal with it on the job. So you want to put forth a positive attitude by showing you can handle some degree of pressure well-enough.
7. Notice how I said *well-enough* and not something like excellent or superb. There is a difference between these three words. And the difference is in degree or the amount of. All an interviewer really needs to see is that you can do the job satisfactorily. *Well-enough* says you can handle it.
8. In other words, it's the difference between being good, very good, excellent, or superb. *Good* means well-enough to succeed, which is the bare minimum. *Very good* is better than good. *Excellent* is beyond very good. And *superb* is above excellent.
9. Part of effective cover letter and resume writing, along with interviewing is the ability to understand how words differ in their degrees and meanings.

Why Work Here?

The key word with this particular question is *here*, meaning this particular company. So with this question, the interviewer is testing your choice selection and decision-making process. This is to determine whether or not you really want to work for them, or are just there because it's work. Now this is where having a more in-depth knowledge of that particular company comes into play.

The more you know about the company, the better you'll be able to explain your exact reason(s) why you feel they are the right fit for you and vice-verse. Any experience with similar companies or industries can help because you'll be able to show that you've worked for others, but like *this* particular company more because …

In other words, you need to look at the company and ask yourself:

→ Why would I be most happy working for them?
→ Exactly how well will I fit-in with them and why?
→ Why would I like to stay and grow with them?

This is what the interviewer really wants from you. A solid and legitimate reason why you feel his or her company is best for you. And specifics do matter! In other words, don't be general because that could send the message you either:

1. Lack any real knowledge about the company
2. Haven't even given it much thought
3. Don't plan on staying very long
4. Don't have a clue what you want

Coming across in any of these ways won't make you look very good. You should also know that most interviewers can spot a BS answer right away! But providing details signals the exact opposite. It tells an interviewer you:

→ Do know about the company
→ Have given it plenty of thought
→ Show good business judgment
→ Were prepared and ready for this question

The bottom-line is:

1. Know enough about the company to say why it's the right one for you. Explain what this particular company offers that really makes you want to join their family and make a career out of it. Also show how you'd like to grow along with them.
2. Believe it yourself or you won't come across as believable. If you don't sound and act as though you honestly feel that way, then no one else will believe it either.
3. Demonstrate why you feel you'll fit-in nicely with the company and it's personnel. Show how your talents will compliment and ultimately benefit them!

Applied or Interviewed Elsewhere?

Now here's a rather interesting question that some applicants will simply refuse to answer on the basis that it's not important. Their attitude will be an interviewer doesn't need to know this information. Others will mention specific companies or jobs. But the real question is what does the interviewer actually want from you? Does he or she want a list of their competitors? The answer is partly yes, but mostly no.

One key thing being tested is whether or not you are in-demand. Not being contacted or interviewed by other companies could imply you're not worth someone else's time. An interviewer may begin to think, "Why should I waste my time too? Well perhaps this company is smarter than the rest. Or it was merely the first one to contact you.

Another thing being tested is your ability to protect information, meaning your ability to hold things in confidence. Does it really matter where you've applied or have been interviewed? No. That's exactly why it isn't necessary to reveal any other companies by name. It's all right to say that there have been others. But what's most important is that you would prefer working for *this* particular company, meaning the interviewer's, most of all!

The last test is whether you know the basic business principle of not putting all your eggs in one basket. Only a fool would pin all hopes on just one place. So it makes perfectly good business sense to have alternatives. Employers realize this and so the interviewer is testing to see if you do too. You need to show the positive traits of planning ahead and having contingency plans. Why? Just in case things don't work out as originally planned.

Your hope is to be hired by this company. But you must still plan for the possibility you may not. So you've applied to others just in case and have ranked your choices in terms of desirability. This illustrates your wise decision-making in action!

The bottom-line is:

1. Mentioning others by name is unnecessary because it's not important. All that matters is you would prefer working for the interviewer's company and are in-demand by others. This is your call to action to the interviewer. You're saying, "Grab me while you can before someone else does!"
2. Show the interviewer that commonsense and good business planning dictate not pinning all your hopes on just one thing. It also involves having alternatives and contingencies. That's because things don't always work out the way one hopes.
3. Explain why you would prefer working there most of all! Be sure you give legitimate reasons because interviewers can pretty easily spot a BS answer.
4. Give the interviewer some *specifics* regarding why you want to work for them. Here is where your knowing lots of information about the company, the job, the profession, and yourself can really come in handy. In other words, the more you know, the better your reasons will be.

5. An interviewer needs some reassurance your preference is to work for them. Even if their company isn't at the top of your list, the interviewer needs the feeling that it is. Otherwise, he or she won't be all that interested in hiring you. Is it smart to hire and train somebody who doesn't really want to work here or in this job or profession? No! This is how an interviewer thinks.

6. Never forget that an interviewer sees you as an investment! So you must come across as being a good one. Someone who plans, shows logical thought, makes wise decisions, and is capable of gathering and assessing information is a good investment. These are the qualities you need to display!

What Makes A Good _____?

More and more interviewers are asking this question today. Let's suppose you're applying for a data entry position. An interviewer might ask you, "What makes a good Data Entry Clerk?" Or something like, "What does it take to be successful in data entry?"

No matter how this question is worded, the interviewer is testing your knowledge of the skills, traits, experience, personality, education, and background needed for success. Translation, it's a test of your ability to research various jobs and fields! Just think about what data entry actually involves:

→ Working more alone and independent
→ Repetition and consistency
→ Being able to accurately and quickly enter lots of information
→ Attention to detail and an ability to remain focused

This is exactly what an interviewer wants to hear in your response. But more important is hearing you possess these abilities! And have either been, or can be effective and successful in this role. In other words, the interviewer wants to know you have a clear understanding of what it takes to be successful in this job and profession.

Having knowledge of the various job duties involved in whatever you're applying for is extremely important to success. Reading multiple job descriptions and speaking with people who've done this sort of work will help. You must show the interviewer that you've researched the field and have some idea as to what qualities it takes to be successful in this job and profession. And what duties and responsibilities jobs in this field generally involve.

Let's look at some other examples so you can get some practice in doing this. Suppose you want to work as a karaoke host. Ask yourself, "What does a karaoke host do?" He or she provides entertainment by allowing people to sing their favorite songs. This requires someone who's extremely good at working with people of varying ages and backgrounds.

It also demands somebody who's very well-organized and can keep track of a constantly changing rotation—a listing of who sings when. You must also make people feel welcome and provide some encouragement to new singers. That means getting the crowd fired up and clapping whenever a singer comes up and has finished. The host also needs to sing when business is slow and field requests from the audience. And because many work in places where alcohol is served (bars, restaurants, and clubs), you may have to contend with a drunken or more rowdy crowd on occasion. Many hosts will even mix karaoke with some dance music. That way, people who don't want to sing won't just have to sit there and listen. They can dance too.

But does it take a college degree? No. Require any formal training? No, it's on-the-job where you learn how to work the system. Must you be able to sing well? Yes. The reason is because if you sing badly then others may be discouraged or feel afraid. Your goal is to provide encouragement, make people feel at ease, and create a fun and exciting atmosphere.

Is there pressure? Yes. People will interrupt you with requests and changes. It may get extremely busy and you won't get to everyone. Are management skills needed? The answer is yes because you'll need to manage the crowd. And decide which of the people who've already sung will go up again. The really good hosts will mix new singers in with the old. That way, everyone feels the host is being fair and trying hard. The bad ones will simply allow their friends and people they know to sing. Or discard songs they don't particularly enjoy.

Now suppose you want to work as a Paralegal or Legal Assistant. What does this person generally do? He or she will research cases and statutes (laws). And prepare various legal documents like pleadings, affidavits, briefs, wills, and contracts. You'll also create files and make copies of things. In addition, you'll do some investigation to determine causes of action or verify facts. And maybe do some arbitration and call witnesses to testify at hearings.

It requires someone having some formal legal training or a strong knowledge of the legal profession. How much training is needed? Well that varies, but a paralegal certificate or Associates Degree is a good start. It also demands somebody who's highly organized and able to meet multiple deadlines. In addition, you must be able to work independently and under tremendous pressure. You must also be able to write well and pay extremely close attention to details. And you have to be extremely good at researching, doing some analysis, and drawing conclusions.

What if you want to be a Barista at Starbucks? A Barista is the one who makes your brewed coffee and espresso. And for those of you who didn't know, there is a difference. But he or she will often do more than just that. In other words, the Barista may also work the cash register, sell pastries and sandwiches, answer customer questions, and stock shelves. This means a Barista needs to be flexible and willing to help out in other areas of the store. And because it can get extremely busy, you must be able to service a large of customers and cope with the pressure.

So you must have excellent time-management, organizational, and multitasking skills. Why? Because you'll be preparing multiple drink orders simultaneously. And you'll need to keep track of different containers and syrups so customer orders aren't mixed-up or prepared incorrectly.

You must also be extremely personable and friendly because you're dealing with the general public. And be able to follow instructions and pay close attention. At many places, you'll notice how the Baristas read back the drink orders before making them. That's to verify they've got it right. With the noise level from the machines and people in the store, sloppy handwriting, and varying drink combinations, accuracy is extremely important!

For instance, one customer way want soy milk while another asks for 2%. Or somebody wants a half a pump of sugar-free raspberry syrup. You must be able to switch gears in an instant. And when it comes to education, most of it is on-the-job training learning the lingo, drinks and ingredients, and store operations. So a high school education is sufficient. However, many are working college students, so there are college-educated employees too.

Let's take someone who wants to work at a car dealership as a Detailer. Detailers are the ones who get the cars cleaned and ready for sale. They'll wash, vacuum, and polish the vehicles. You'll need to work in all kinds of weather, tend to work alone, and have a section or given number of cars to service. Careful attention must be paid to preventing damages from occurring. As for education, high school is perfectly acceptable. In other words, it's mainly routine and very labor-intensive, not rocket science. And involves the use of cleaning products and equipment. So on-the-job training is really all that's needed.

Our final example will be someone who wants to work as a Payroll Clerk. This person's main function is to pay employees. Now depending on how large a company or office, it can be a small or large payroll. But regardless, it requires someone who's extremely accurate and can meet deadlines. The last thing you want is an employee not getting paid on-time or receiving the wrong amount. So you must be very detail-oriented. You also have to be good with numbers and double-checking accuracy. And should be very good at ten-key (typing numbers) by touch. With ten-key, there's typing *by sight* or *by touch*. The difference is that *by sight* mean you need to look at the keys, which slows you down. *By touch* means you don't need to look at the number or keypad, which speeds you up.

For instance, maybe an employee added-up his or her hours wrong. You'll need to make the adjustment so that employee is paid the correct amount. And you'll need to understand the various deductions that can be made. As far as education goes, a college degree isn't absolutely necessary. Many get trained on-the-job. But others will have an accounting certificate or Associates Degree. And there is the CPP certification that designates you as a *Certified Payroll Professional*. Some will obtain this to show they've been trained or specialize in handling payroll.

The bottom-line is:

1. Know what various jobs or job categories typically involve. Ask yourself, "What does someone in this job or field generally do?" Answering this requires you to do some research and homework. So an interviewer is testing your ability to conduct research.
2. Ask yourself, "What type of person is needed to be successful in this job and profession?" Identify the characteristics and desirable qualities one needs in order to do a good job and be effective in it. In other words, correctly identify what skills, personality, experience, education, etc would be needed in general.
3. Demonstrate and explain that you possess several, if not most or all of these same qualities. This will link success with you! If you don't possess these, then show you are fully capable of learning and mastering those needed qualities pretty easily and quickly. And show you're willing to learn and want to be successful!

Tip: An excellent strategy is to use someone else as an example of what's not effective or good. Then contrast this person with yourself. The purpose is to show how you—the effective and good one—differ from the other who is not.

4. For example, it's all right to say you've worked for or with someone who wasn't very good at say relating to customers. As a result, those customers didn't overly like this person. But they liked you because you had a nice rapport with them and provided quality service. This way, you're not badmouthing anyone. You're merely pointing-out the differences between someone who's good, meaning you, and someone who isn't. You're also stressing the fact that you are very good at what you do!

What Motivates You?

Here is another good question because it gets straight to the heart of your personality. And that's exactly what's being tested. With this question, the interviewer is looking at three things:

1. What type of person you are
2. How well you'll fit-in
3. If you're merely applying because you need a job, meaning any job

By examining your motivation, an interviewer can learn a great deal about you as a person. Are you driven by:

→ Money or power?
→ A love of the job or profession?
→ Your hopes of achieving fame and glory?
→ The prospects of moving-up the ladder?
→ The advice of others, meaning relatives, friends, teachers, etc?

Your answer could be the deciding factor between landing this job or not. But more importantly is what the interviewer *perceives* as your true motivation. So think hard before speaking! Here are your keys to success:

KEY #1:   Discuss why you like this profession.

KEY #2:   Explain why you want this job, at this company.

KEY #3:   Show how it definitely fits-in with your career goals!

For example, many people working in sales are driven mainly or entirely by the money. Now being money-driven is all right up to a point. But an interviewer prefers hiring someone who truly enjoys, or feels he or she would enjoy sales. Someone who really wants to be a part of that profession and wants to work *here*, instead of just anywhere or somewhere else. If the interviewer gets the feeling your only motivation is money, then he or she may begin to wonder if you'll "up and leave" should a higher paying job come along. So don't raise that potential red flag here.

The bottom-line is:

1. Know something about the job itself and the profession as a whole, including what successful traits are needed. This way, you can link your personality and background to the job and profession. Explain how we have a good match between yourself, the profession, and the job.
2. You want the interviewer believing you're cutout for this field and job. Making this connection perfectly clear is an excellent way of dong this.
3. Show your desire to join this particular company, in this job, and that it is what you want. Also explain how it will help you get to where you want to be.
4. Don't dwell on money! Money is nothing more than a reward for doing well, and is not a substitute for happiness. Hence the expression, "Money can't buy happiness."
5. It's a given that money is important to you. But you want the interviewer to see your primary motivation is something other than money. This way, the interviewer won't begin to feel you'll simply move on to another job the moment you're offered more money. Money-driven people are never satisfied and will tend to jump at opportunities involving even more money or power.
6. You main motivation has to be something positive so you appear as though you want to work in this job and profession! This makes you a wise investment and more likely to stay with the company longer. In other words, your motivation is to learn, grow, and become successful.
7. But what if you're interviewing for a job you have no intention in keeping very long? Or don't plan on making a career out of it? In other words, "Any job will do." How should you handle this situation?

Tip: You don't want the interviewer to know you don't plan on staying or making a career out of it. That will kill your chances of success! You must explain that you fully-intend on giving them 100% effort to do well.

Greatest Accomplishment

The key word here is *greatest*, meaning the one you are most proud of. Just like all the other interview questions we've covered so far, you are again being tested. But this time, the test is three-fold:

1. Do you have any accomplishments?
2. If so, which is your best and why?
3. Do you take and show pride in a job well-done?

Your answers can reveal a great deal about your personality. And that's exactly why interviewers like this question. Anyone who lacks pride and accomplishments is not really somebody employers want on their teams. No matter what job it is, pride in your own work with a feeling of "I did good!" is super important. This is what the interviewer is really driving at. So whatever accomplishment you pick, make sure it's something an interviewer would say, "You should be proud of that!" And show your enthusiasm in both your voice and body language.

Some experts advise not choosing an accomplishment that's somewhat or totally unrelated to the job you're applying for. But I disagree with them and here's why. Anything good you've done and are proud of makes you look impressive because you're displaying the qualities an interviewer is looking for in your response—Being proud of something good you've done!

For example, you applied for a job as a Paralegal and your proudest moment was when you performed on stage in a school play. In my professional opinion, you still look good. As long as you smile and your eyes light-up when you talk about it, you're demonstrating the positive trait of taking pride in doing well.

Yes, I agree that performing in a play has nothing to do with working in the legal profession. Yet being proud of what you've accomplished in your life or on the job is something that crosses over into anything else. You're still telling an interviewer you feel you did something noteworthy and are darn proud of it. That's exactly what the interviewer wants to hear!

However, I do agree that mentioning an accomplishment more closely related to the job or profession is better. But using something unrelated won't necessarily hurt your chances. The point is the interviewer must see your pride, enthusiasm, and why that particular accomplishment ranks #1.

> **Tip**: If you overcame a drug, alcohol, or mental problem, spent time in jail, or ended-up with the wrong crowd, you can turn this to your advantage.

How? By mentioning how proud you are that you turned your life around. And how you're a much better person today because of this. This highlights your taking initiative to deal with a problem, overcoming a huge challenge, and making a very wise decision. You look impressive here because not everybody in your situation would be able to turn his or her life around. But you did!

The bottom-line is:

1. Have a very specific accomplishment in mind beforehand and don't be afraid to talk about it.
2. Be sure you show genuine enthusiasm and pride while speaking. This will match your emotion to your words, making you more believable.
3. Explain why you're so proud of this accomplishment so the interviewer can see your thought process in action.
4. Explain how pride in that accomplishment illustrates your overall attitude of taking pride in doing a good job. This says you'll not only do good work, but will be proud of it too. In other words, pride and good work go hand-in-hand!

Favorite Job

This question, and all its variations is another test of your personality, thought process, and decision-making. An interviewer wants to know the specific job you feel was your favorite or most enjoyable. But more importantly, why!

> **KEY**:   An interviewer wants specifics, not generalities!

Explain why this particular job rates higher than any other. And make sure your answer is something the interviewer will say to himself or herself, "I can see (understand) why you chose that one."

In other words, an interviewer wants to know what elements of the job appealed most to you. For example, was it:

→ How you were treated by management, staff, customers, etc?
→ The nature of the work?
→ The training you received or opportunities available?
→ The corporate culture?
→ Flexibility?
→ The range of duties or job responsibilities you had?

> **Tip**:   Don't say it was the money!

This implies you didn't care for the work itself. Nor did you enjoy the people with whom you worked, the profession, etc. No, the only thing you enjoyed was the money, and that can utterly destroy you in an interview!. To be successful here, you must focus on the positive things an interviewer can, and will, respect.

The bottom-line is:

1. Know in advance what you liked and disliked about each of your jobs, including your current or most recent one. This shows anticipation of this question and you'll be ready for it.
2. Showcase your ability to rank your jobs from best to worst.
3. Be specific in terms of why you chose a particular job as your most favorite or enjoyable.
4. When talking, show enthusiasm and smile. After all, you're suppose to be talking about your best job. Failure to display these when discussing a good thing signals you are lying and really didn't enjoy it.
5. What if you chose a job that's unrelated to what you're interviewing for? For example, picking a construction job when you're applying for a hotel front desk position. In this case, you must explain why you'd be happy working the front desk.
6. It's important you make the connection between what makes you happy and this job or field. Otherwise, the interviewer will be asking why you're here when what really makes you happy is something else. That's why it's so important to explain what aspects of this job make you happy.

Least Favorite Job

This question is very similar to the previous one asking about your favorite job. The difference here is that you're being tested on whether you'll speak badly about your current or previous employer.

Tip #1: Never badmouth any of your current or previous employers!

This means not roasting the people with whom you worked, the company, nor any of it's personnel or policies. In other words, you don't want to go overboard with any criticisms.

For example, telling an interviewer you worked for someone who was a real SOB makes you look rather mean. I suggest toning it down by perhaps focusing on this person's ineffectiveness, poor managerial or customer relation skills, etc.

By handling it this way, you're not insulting or badmouthing anyone. You're using sound business judgment to justify why you weren't happy. The interviewer will appreciate you're not saying anything overly negative. Otherwise, the interviewer may think you'd say very negative things about his or her company if you were to leave.

Tip #2: Never mention anyone in particular by name!

The reason why is because you don't know who the interviewer knows. For all you know, the interviewer might know this person and like him or her. In addition, you're embarrassing this person in front of a total stranger—the interviewer. And this makes you seem rather nasty.

The key here is to display solid business judgment and logical reasoning. Feel free to explain things like:

- ➜ Disagreements over policies
- ➜ Personality conflicts
- ➜ Lack of growth
- ➜ Changes in job responsibilities

Explain how the work environment wasn't a pleasant one. Or wasn't what you had hoped or wanted it to be. This way, the interviewer can relate and understand why you weren't happy there. A true professional will always be respectful and never criticize someone by name or ruin anybody's reputation. This is how you must behave in order to be successful.

Tip #3: Don't say a company policy or anyone in particular was stupid or dumb!

Once again, you appear very mean, which severely hurts your chances of success. I suggest you tone it down by saying something more along the lines of how a policy made things harder. For example, increasing the amount of paperwork to complete, duplicating stuff, etc. Or why you felt someone wasn't very effective or reliable.

This way, you're using sound business reasoning to explain why that work environment wasn't the nicest in comparison to your others. You're simply explaining why this particular job, at this particular company, wasn't the best in comparison to the others you've had. Now this doesn't automatically mean you hated working there. It's just when looking back over all your jobs, this particular one happens to rank lowest.

For example, I worked at one place where I was promoted from supporting Sales Managers to supporting the Director of Sales. This included some added responsibilities I thoroughly enjoyed. But when my boss left the company shortly thereafter, the new Director came in and took all those added responsibilities I enjoyed so much away. Something that made my job far less enjoyable and left practically no room for advancement. So I decided to leave.

The point I'm making is that your least favorite, or worst job, doesn't have to be something you hated. It could simply be the job became less enjoyable. In my case, the job went from exciting and having potential for upward mobility, to more boring and stagnant. So the unpleasantness wasn't that I didn't like my new boss or the job. It was the opportunity for career growth and greater responsibilities had suddenly been taken away.

But this wasn't the case in another one of my past jobs. My boss would yell and scream at the staff, myself included, right in front of our customers. In fact, one of my customers had even asked me how I could work for someone like that day in and day out. Well let me tell you it wasn't very easy! I literally dreaded going into work each day and just couldn't wait to get out and find something better.

So your reason(s) for putting a company or job on your worst list could be that it really was a terrible experience. Or it could be the job wasn't as pleasant as your others. Either way, an interviewer wants to see how you think and evaluate things. And if you can demonstrate solid business thinking and judgment.

The bottom-line is:

1. Never roast or badmouth any of your employers, including their employees and policies!
2. Do feel free to discuss how the overall work environment wasn't as nice or pleasant as the others you've had. And exactly why you feel this way.
3. Show the employer that you've thought carefully about it, and honestly feel getting out of there was the right decision.

Salary

The question of how much you want in terms of salary seems pretty straightforward, right? Wrong, it's another test. But this time it's on your abilities to conduct some research, gather information, and plan ahead.

An interviewer really wants to know if you have a good idea what jobs like this even pay. Or better yet, what they'd pay in this specific geographic region. Now if you've done your homework and have current, up-to-date information, then you should be able to provide a figure that's in the ballpark. Some helpful resources I suggest you look at include:

→ Your local newspaper or the one where you'll be seeking work. I suggest looking at them over time to see if there's a trend in salaries. Do they appear to be holding steady? Falling? Increasing? Also look at multiple categories where you think ads might appear. For instance, bank jobs can be found in sections like: Banking, Finance, Financial Services, Sales, Customer Service, and Management or Management Trainee.

→ *www.salary.com*. If they don't have figures for your local area, then try to find a nearby major city or geographic region. And use those figures as your guide. Be sure you look at related jobs too! The reason is because the site lists information by job title. And they can vary widely from company to company.

→ Employment or staffing agencies. Search their ads and website to see what salaries they're currently offering. And realize some of those salaries may be lower than direct-hire by individual companies. It's because sales commission and overhead costs are sometimes factored in. Not always the case, but just something to keep in mind and understand.

Tip #1: If you're thinking of, or will be relocating to another state, then you may want to visit the U.S. Department of Labor's website (*www.dol.gov*). They have a wealth of information on labor market conditions and minimum wage information for each state (*www.dol.gov/esa*).

For example, Texas and Kentucky have state minimums equal to the federal minimum wage. Others, like Washington and Florida, have minimums higher than the federal. Alabama and Tennessee have no state minimum wage. And Georgia and Kansas have minimums lower than the federal.

In addition, minimum wage increases vary in amount and timing. For example, Washington State raised its minimum by 14 cents to $8.07 per hour effective January 1, 2008. This makes them the highest in the nation! California raised its minimum by 50 cents on January 1, 2008 to $8 per hour. North Carolina will increase theirs by 40 cents to $6.55 on July 24, 2008. And Ohio's minimum as of January 1, 2008 became $7 per hour.

So how should you handle the question of salary? Well I've come across a number of experts who advise you not provide a salary figure at all for two main reasons. First, you may not know what the job actually pays and could mention a figure that's either too low or too high. Secondly, any discussion regarding salary should be reserved until later in the hiring process. In other words, it shouldn't be discussed until you're closer to being offered, or have been offered the job. Right now, you're only interviewing and not being offered anything. In addition, there are others who advise you should actually throw it back at the interviewer by saying something like "Are you offering me the job?"

But I look at it this way. To an employer, salary is an important factor in deciding whether to hire an applicant. So asking how much you want is relevant and important. And so from an interviewer's standpoint, it's important to gain a sense of how much an applicant is looking for to see if it's even in my acceptable pay range. An applicant's refusal to address the salary issue could raise these questions in the mind of an interviewer:

- ➔ What are you afraid of?
- ➔ What's the matter, don't you have some idea how much you want or are worth?
- ➔ Do you have any clue what jobs like this pay?
- ➔ Are you just willing to blindly accept whatever I offer you?
- ➔ Do you think you're not worth being paid for your time and hard work?

My point is you wouldn't be job hunting if you didn't need work and more importantly money. So it's just commonsense you'd have a salary figure in mind while looking. After all, you know how much you need to live on and make ends meet, so you must a salary in mind. These are all the things that will run through an interviewer's head. So you must address them to make yourself look good!

Tip #2:   Don't give a single dollar amount nor refuse to answer!

Instead, present the interviewer with an acceptable salary range based upon your solid researching. Continue on to explain that you're more interested in the job or nature of the work and the satisfaction you'll get from doing it, as opposed to the money. In other words, you *de-emphasize* the money issue! And focus more on your desire to find a job that fits-in with your goals and will make you happy. At the same time, you give the interviewer a clear idea what you want in terms of money. This shows you've thought things through and are a real professional!

If you feel you deserve closer to the high-end of your salary range, or perhaps even more, then you can explain your reason(s) why. After all, an interview is all about selling yourself! Providing a legitimate reason why you deserve more than another is something an interviewer will take under advisement. Now this doesn't mean he or she will agree to it. Merely the interviewer will consider it if it sounds reasonable and justifiable.

For example, if the range is $10-11.50 and you feel you deserve closer to $13 because you have double the experience of the typical applicant, then say so. By doing this, you're showing confidence, logical thinking, and foresight, which are all positives. Then again, it's quite possible an interviewer will respond by actually saying or giving-off a signal—body language—that it's above what they'd be willing to pay.

And this is exactly why I suggest you tell the interviewer that doing the kind of work you enjoy, and earning enough to live on, is more important to you than the money itself. This way, you've allayed the interviewer's fears that you're only in it for the money. You're also being flexible and reasonable. Furthermore, you're standing-up and saying "I'm worth it!" without being far beyond their acceptable range.

In other words, you've:

➔ Shown confidence that you're worth the money and are a wise investment
➔ Provided a rational explanation why you deserve more
➔ Demonstrated solid researching by knowing what your competition would be like and what jobs like this pay
➔ Drawn attention to the fact you're looking for a rewarding job that's personally satisfying

An interviewer can't help but respect and admire you now because you're coming across as somebody who knows what he or she is worth. And someone who can justify it using sound reasoning. Now there is an alternative strategy and one I've used myself. This second approach involves your asking the interviewer directly if he or she could provide you with an idea what the job pays. You then let him or her know if this is within your acceptable range.

With this second approach, you're getting the pay rate directly from the interviewer *before* you respond. Some may find this useful because it can prevent you from low-balling yourself. Now some interviewers will respond favorably by giving you a range or a very specific figure. Others will say nothing more than, "What would you like?"

If you get the latter, meaning the interviewer asks you how much you want, then go back to approach #1 and state your acceptable range. How well does this second approach work? Well I had an interviewer who stated a salary range *higher* than mine! Which method you ultimately decide to use is strictly a matter of personal choice. So feel free to pick the one you feel most comfortable with. Or vary your approach to see if one works better.

The bottom-line is:

1. *Never* refuse to answer nor ask the interviewer if you're being offered the job. Refusing to answer doesn't make any sense because you're job hunting. And so you must have some idea how much you want to be paid.
2. If you were being offered the job, you'd know it because the interviewer would tell you directly. And you're being very presumptuous by asking if he or she is offering you the job right now. That doesn't make you look good because you could have guessed wrong.
3. You don't know what they will or won't do. You're also failing to realize that in most cases, an interview doesn't end with a job offer. It ends with a smaller number of candidates to consider. There's usually some discussion afterwards in order to decide who fits best and can do the job.
4. Have a good sense what jobs like this might pay by doing your homework. Then give a *realistic* salary range based upon it. Use resources like your local paper, job boards, job postings, college career centers, etc. Look for differences in the amount or level of experience, education, and other qualifications to see where you'd probably fit-in.
5. Be confident in terms of your salary expectations and reason(s) because this shows the interviewer you honestly feel you're worth every penny!

6. Explain that money is *not* the most important thing to you, but you obviously need enough to make ends meet and live.

7. Emphasize you care more about doing the kind of work you enjoy and doing it well. And you welcome the opportunity to work there and grow with them. In other words, you're placing job satisfaction and your happiness *above* money! This makes you a better investment because you'll tend to stay longer if you like what you're doing or enjoy the profession.

8. Let the interviewer know that all you're really after is the chance to prove yourself. And you have every confidence in your ability to perform well and fit-in nicely if they give you that chance!

Who You Most Admire

This may seem like one of those unusual questions an interviewer might ask. But believe me when I say that it does have a very specific purpose. And just like a more standard question, it's testing something. This time, it's your personality that's being tested by asking what type of person you consider to be a role-model. For example, is it:

- → An athlete?
- → A celebrity?
- → A member of your family?
- → One of your friends or a friend of the family?
- → A current or former co-worker or supervisor?
- → A politician or world leader?
- → A religious leader?
- → A book or movie character?
- → A current or former teacher?

Your choice can reveal a great deal about the qualities you find most admirable in a person. It can also help an interviewer determine how well you'll fit-in and interact with company personnel and customers.

KEY: The person you select must exhibit the positive qualities an interviewer will like and respect

This means it should be somebody who has positively affected you as a person or as a worker. You must then be able to clearly explain how this person has positively influenced you. Briefly say why this person is *worthy* of your utmost respect and admiration. In other words, make it clear to the interviewer why you feel this person is a good role-model.

Tip: Avoid religious leaders or anyone potentially controversial

Now don't get me wrong, I have nothing whatsoever against religion. I only make this suggestion because religion can be a deeply personal thing to many people. Some have prejudices about other religions. Others have no religious affiliations. And many believe religion and the workplace should remain totally separate.

In addition, you could run into an interviewer who pictures you preaching to others. Or conflicting with others who may not share your faith or devotion. So in my opinion, you could be opening a can of worms that's best left closed.

However, if you're applying to a religious or religious-affiliated institution, company, or organization, then it may be appropriate to mention a religious figure or leader. For example, someone who is interviewing at a Church may say that he or she most admires the Pope. Someone applying to a Jewish organization could mention someone like Abraham or Moses. My advice here would be to focus on the positive qualities within that person and not preach the gospel.

The reason why I suggest avoiding potentially controversial individuals is because it might be someone who the interviewer doesn't particularly like or admire. For example, some of us have very strong opinions and attitudes regarding President George W. Bush. Some really like him; others utterly despise or hate him. And some don't believe or trust him. So choosing President Bush may not be your best choice given the wide range of attitudes and opinions towards him.

But no matter whom you choose, it's your decision! I simply prefer to avoid potential conflict or red flags. Remember, your ultimate goal here is to make it past the interviewer. And mentioning someone controversial could make this harder. So all I ask is you consider this in making your selection.

The bottom-line is:

1. Choose someone who has had a positive influence on your life or work.
2. Explain how this person has greatly influenced you so the interviewer can see your reasoning and say, "I can understand why you chose that person." In other words, make the connection between the person you chose and yourself. This will illustrate how that person has been like a mentor to you.
3. Be sure the person you choose exhibits the positive qualities an employer will like. Don't pick anyone shady or criminal where the interviewer will say, "That's no role model!"
4. For example, Bernie Ebbers wouldn't be a good choice if you're applying for an accounting position. He was the former head of WorldComm who's serving prison time for accounting fraud. You want to be seen as ethical and trustworthy. He's the exact opposite!
5. Due to possible prejudices and other potential problems, I suggest staying away from religious figures and anyone who might be viewed as controversial. My job here is to help improve your chances of success, which is why I make this suggestion. However, the choice is yours to make!
6. It's perfectly all right to choose a fictional character instead of an actual person. That is as long as the fictional character exhibits positive qualities to be admired. There are plenty of literary, cartoon, and movie characters that some might see as role-models.
7. But in my professional opinion, I suggest picking somebody *real* instead of fictional. The reason is because an interviewer may think you don't feel there's any good human role-model. And this might hurt your chances.
8. An interviewer might say that with all the living and deceased people throughout history, somebody must be a role-model in your opinion. But as I mentioned earlier, choosing a fictional character wouldn't be wrong. So the final decision is yours to make.

Leader or Follower?

This particular question gets right to the heart of a candidate's personality, and that is exactly what an interviewer is testing. In other words, the interviewer is trying to determine which category you fall into:

➜ **Leader**: Someone who takes charge or shows imitative
➜ **Follower**: One who doesn't take charge and merely does what others ask

But your personality isn't the only thing being tested. An interviewer is also gauging your decision-making ability. And the way it's being tested is by giving you very specific choices from which to choose. The interviewer is extremely interested in seeing how you arrived at your decision. And will be deciding whether or not he or she agrees it. In addition, an interviewer is testing your researching skills.

  KEY #1: Look and sound the part!

The most important thing is for you to look and sound like your answer. Let's use an example to illustrate. Suppose you're interviewing a potential new hire and ask that person the following question: "Do you consider yourself to be a leader or a follower?" The candidate's response is, "I feel that I'm a leader."

Let's further assume this person has been completely honest with you up to this point. So there's no reason to question it here, right? But does this automatically mean you would agree with the candidate's assertion he or she is a leader? I did say that person has been honest all along, so why you would question it?

The *key* lies in the candidate's voice and body language! For example, suppose the answer was spoken in a more quiet and softer voice. Would you consider someone who doesn't speak-up to be a leader? The answer is no! A leader need to be heard and sound as though they're in-charge. So a more commanding and powerful voice is necessary.

Now suppose the answer was spoken in a more normal or louder voice. Would this sound more like a leader? The answer is yes! Leaders speak so their subordinates can hear and understand them. So a leadership voice is a more powerful one that says "I'm in-charge and have something to say."

  Tip #1: There's a difference between a "leadership" voice and one too loud or powerful

As I just mentioned, a leader needs to have a more powerful voice. But it shouldn't be one that so loud it hurts one's ears. An exception would be a military drill sergeant. Here, yelling out commands is quite common because you're outside, dealing with large numbers of subordinates, and may be simulating battlefield conditions. But outside of the military, a slightly more powerful voice is what's needed. In other words, you want one that people can easily hear and understand. Speaking-up is all right; screaming is not!

Let's now focus on body language. What if the candidate was looking down while speaking? Does that exhibit leadership behavior? No! And that's because a leader doesn't look away. By looking away, you're conveying a sense of fear or nervousness. A leader is unafraid and confident!

The point I'm making is that an interviewer will often match your words to your body language and tone of voice. If you don't appear to be what your words are saying, then the interviewer won't be convinced you're really that way. The interviewer may think you're lying or don't really believe what you're saying. And this can hurt your chances!

KEY #2:   Know the job and the profession

By knowing more about the job itself and the profession as a whole, you can better gauge whether it would require a more leadership-type person or not. For example, in management, leadership is crucial to success. A manager—in any company and at any level—makes decisions! So displaying leadership is just a given and goes with the territory. Part of what an interviewer is doing is testing your understand of this.

Someone who applies for a managerial position and says he or she is a follower would not impress me. Why not? Because that applicant failed to realize that management, by its very nature, demands someone who is more of a leader. This is where an interviewer tests your researching skills and knowledge of the profession as a whole!

KEY #3:   **Followers beware**: Leadership is sometimes important

When people interview for support positions like Administrative Assistant, Customer Service Representative, Office Clerk, they'll often make a mistake by saying they're followers. So what's wrong with this? These jobs only provide support to superiors and don't involve making decisions or taking charge, right? Wrong!

Yes, your primary role in jobs like this is more following the direction of your boss. However, you may also make some decisions! In other words, it definitely takes more of a follower, but it also may require someone capable of making decisions and taking some action.

For example, let's say that an angry customer calls you on the phone to complain about something, but your boss is either out of the office or unavailable at the moment. What would you do in this situation? Would you:

→ Get someone else to help?
→ Take a message and leave it for your boss?
→ Try to help this person yourself?
→ Refuse to help anybody who's angry or unpleasant?

The point I'm making is that something needs to be done. And it's up to you to *decide* what that is. This puts you in the position of having to take charge and function as a leader. While this may not be a very high-level, nor even the most important decision, it's still a decision. And you are the one who has to deal with the consequences if you make the wrong decision. So an interviewer needs to see you exhibit some leadership qualities in addition your mainly being in a supportive role. If you plan on rising higher up the ladder, then it's even more important to show some imitative and leadership qualities.

KEY #4:   **Leaders beware**: Following is sometimes important

Just like a support person needs to have some leadership qualities, a leader needs some follower qualities too. You see, managers report to somebody else who supervises or overseas their work. This means you may be taking some direction from the person above you. And that puts you in the role of a follower.

For example, a Sales Manager may report to the Regional or District Manager. A Manufacturing Manger might report to the Vice President. A Vice President may report to the President. Even a Chief Executive Office (CEO) is accountable in some degree to the Board of Directors. In other words, most managers can't just do whatever they want. They have a boss too!

The bottom-line:

1. Research whether that particular job or profession requires someone who is more of a leader, or more of a follower. This way, you'll know walking in the door which way the interviewer is leaning. I suggest looking closely at the job description and knowing more about what that job or profession would typically involve.
2. If the job or profession appears to more supportive in nature, then it would lean towards needing a follower. But if the job is more supervisory or managerial in nature, then it would need more of a leader.
3. Regardless of whether you consider yourself to be more of a leader or a follower, understand that most, if not all jobs require some combination of both.
4. I suggest telling an interviewer which category—leader or follower—best describes you. Then continue on to explain that you exhibit some qualities from the other category. This way, you show an understanding that many jobs and professions need elements of both in order to be successful.
5. You may think of yourself as being more of one or the other. But you also are smart enough to realize that leaders may need to follow from time-to-time. And followers might have to take the lead on occasion.
6. Look and act the role! It is absolutely crucial that you behave in an appropriate manner here. When talking about your leadership qualities, you need to look and sound like a leader. This means speaking-up, speaking with confidence, and not looking away.

Tip #2:   Any *specific* situation you can present to demonstrate your leadership is helpful

7. Even for those of you who are followers or will be providing support. *Briefly* tell the interviewer exactly how you took charge, showed initiative, or made a wise decision. And be prepared to go into more details if the interviewer asks. This way, you're not just saying it, you're proving it!

Ever Been Fired?

If you ask people who've been fired (terminated, let go) before this question, I think most would probably be afraid to say "yes." Especially during an interview where your goal is to make yourself look good. Admitting you were fired doesn't seem to do this. Or does it?

It all boils down to the reason(s) behind your termination. For example, being let go for something like insubordination can definitely make you look very bad! In fact, unemployment benefits may even be *denied* in some states if you were insubordinate. Yet being terminated isn't necessarily a bad thing. And despite the belief by many that it's the end of the world, it doesn't have to be. As I mentioned earlier, it all hinges on the reason(s) why you were let go.

For example, people get fired due to budget cuts, downsizing, outsourcing, or a change in management. Will being terminated for these reasons make you look bad to an interviewer? No. And that's because it wasn't your fault. It was something was beyond your control.

My point is that being let go, in and of itself, doesn't automatically hurt your chances for success. And that applies even if you did something to get yourself fired. You see, employers realize there may come a point where a good and successful employee simply lost his or her job due to reasons beyond control. An interviewer is testing whether or not you were a victim of this. And if so, are you bitter, angry, or brooding over it? Or did you simply accept it and move on with your life?

Let's assume that you were fired at some point in your career. The most important thing to an interviewer is how you handled yourself afterwards. This is another thing being tested. For instance, did you:

→ Change your ways and learn from your mistake(s)?
→ Just move on to the next job?
→ Change fields or careers?
→ Get discouraged and stop looking for work altogether?
→ Badmouth the one who terminated you, the company, or any of their employees?
→ Try to convince others to quit

To an interviewer, the ability to learn and grow from past mistakes is taken as a positive! We're all human. And human beings will make a mistake at one time or another.

KEY: Learn from past mistakes!

A candidate who was fired and didn't learn from that experience will be seen as somebody who's unable to change. And as a result, more likely to repeat that mistake. Or someone who'll make a similar mistake in the future. These won't make you look good in the mind of an interviewer. But if can show the interviewer you

have learned from that experience and won't make the same mistake again, then the interviewer will see you in a more positive light.

The bottom-line is:

1. Being fired isn't necessarily a bad thing. Many people have been let go and became successful later on.
2. An interviewer is more interested in whether or not you learned something from your having been fired.
3. If you were fired for something that *wasn't* your fault, such as departmental or budgetary cutbacks, then it's all right to admit you were fired. This happens to many people and isn't that unusual.
4. Companies may have to let good people go because revenue isn't so great Maybe the company is in serious financial trouble and has to let people go in order to recover. Or a management change resulted in restructuring.
5. My point is that good and valued employees may be terminated or laid-off during economic downturns or in times of crisis. So it may have nothing to do with poor performance or messing-up. Interviewers understand this!
6. What if you were fired for something major that really was your fault? It's absolutely critical to show the interviewer you learned from that mistake. This way, the interviewer will realize you made a stupid mistake back then. And have learned not to do it again. This puts you in a more positive light and increases your chances for success!
7. Showing an interviewer the capacity to grow and learn from a bad experience is taken as a positive. Human's aren't perfect and occasionally mistakes. What's important is learning from them so we don't repeat them. The same goes for having a bad experience. We don't want to put ourselves in that situation again, so we do our best avoid it.

When Can You Start?

This question seems very simple. Just give the interviewer the date when you can actually start. But hold on, not so fast! The key to handling this question hinges on that date. You see, part of what an interviewer is testing is whether or not you understand the common business courtesy of giving two weeks notice.

If you're currently employed, can you just "up and leave," meaning quit? Sure, you could just leave your present job and begin the new one. But would your old boss be very happy about this? Do you think he or she would give your new employer a good reference? No!

Some of you may not know this, but it wouldn't be unusual for employers to check a new employee's references until after he or she has started. One reason is you're not human resource's biggest priority. So they may not get around to it until after you've started and completed all your paperwork. It could also take several tries to contact your references.

In addition, if you were to simply quit your present job, the interviewer may begin to wonder if you'll do the same thing if they hired you. He or she will imagine your getting a better job offer and leaving. So all that time and money invested in you would essentially be wasted. And lastly, quitting a job right away could put the old employer in a tough spot because you're leaving them in a lurch. Remember, the workplace doesn't just stop. So they'd have to find someone to do your work very quickly. This makes their life tougher because your leaving came more unexpectedly. And that leaves less time to adjust and work around it.

> **KEY**: Explain that you are not the type of person who leaves a job without giving a reasonable amount of time for them to adjust. Giving two weeks notice is standard.

What if the interviewer or new employer asks you to begin "sooner," meaning earlier than two weeks? Here's my three-step strategy for handing this:

1. Mention that you would prefer starting a little later so you don't leave your current boss in a bind
2. Ask for permission to give more notice
3. If the interviewer won't agree to additional time, then let him or her know that you'd be willing to work around their schedule by giving less notice

This way, you show a willingness to do what the interviewer wants. You just didn't want to make it overly tough on your current boss. That's perfectly understandable and something the interviewer will appreciate. Now you're behaving like a true professional. The interviewer will now decide whether or not to honor your request. If so, wonderful. But if not, then you'll need to work around the new employer.

Tip #1: Suppose you decide to accept the job and the interviewer refuses to grant you this extra time. Make sure your current boss knows you would have liked to give more notice. But unfortunately, your new employer needs you to start earlier.

My approach lets your current boss know it wasn't your idea to leave sooner. It was merely that the new employer needs you earlier and you have no choice but to work around them. Even if your current boss doesn't particularly like this, he or she will respect you and realize it wasn't your decision. In other words, it was something beyond your control. This makes you look extremely professional, friendly, and helpful. Now you'll be able to leave on good terms and get a nice recommendation.

But what if you're not currently employed and working. Is it then all right to say you're available right away or 'immediately? The answer is still no! In an interviewer's mind, he or she might think you have no other job prospects and are merely jumping at this one Besides, you may want to take some time to think it over and make absolutely sure it's the right job and company for you.

In both life and the workplace, it's always best to think before you act! The interviewer is testing your understanding of this. So he or she needs to see you don't jump at something without first weighing the pros and cons. You also want to send the message their company isn't the only one on your platter. Why? Because you believe in your abilities and know another would be glad to have you.

This makes you look more attractive because the interviewer will think others may be interested in hiring you. In other words, I'm suggesting you convey the message you are in demand by others. And that you don't jump at something without first giving it some thought. How much time do you need to think it over? I would say a couple of days to a week is sufficient.

The bottom-line is:

1. Giving your current employer two weeks notice when quitting is considered an industry standard. It's also customary to write a letter of resignation and hand it to your boss.
2. A letter of resignation is generally short and sweet. It lets the employer know the exact date when you'll be leaving, and your reason(s).
3. It's also best to sit down with your boss and explain why you'll be leaving. Then hand him or her your letter. In other words, you don't just slide it under the door or stick it in his or her mailbox. The reason is because some would consider that unprofessional, cold, or mean. You want to be remembered as a true professional who leaves the right way!

Tip #2: Be nice in your letter! Remember, it goes into your permanent file and may make the difference between getting a good or a bad reference. Especially for those of you who are quitting a job you hate. Or where you aren't particularly liked by others.

4. Doing the nice thing shows you don't harbor ill will. And that bumps you up a notch. Maybe just enough to get yourself a decent recommendation, which is better than bad one. Or even worse, none at all!
5. If you have a job now and the interviewer wants you to start earlier than two weeks, don't fight it. Instead, let the interviewer know that you would prefer giving your current boss more time so they aren't left in a bind. This shows you're mindful of the need not to just up and quit without giving

appropriate notice. However, you do have to work around the new employer. So be nice in asking for additional time to start.

6. If you're not working and are asked to begin right away or the next day, you may want to ask for more time to think it over. It's pretty common to ask for about a week to think things over. This way, you can weight the pros and cons, see if you hear from any others, or even contact others and let them know you have another offer and need to let them know quickly.

Handling Conflict or Problems

This question gets right to the heart of your problem-solving and conflict resolution skills. And that's exactly what an interviewer is testing. Now some applicants make an interview mistake by saying they've never had a conflict in their entire life. This is mainly done because they're afraid. Afraid that saying yes will make them look bad in the eyes of the interviewer. But interviewers realize that some degree of conflict, be it minor or major, can happen in the workplace and in one's own personal life.

For example, it could be a little thing. Everybody but you wants to go out after work and your co-workers are trying to convince you to join them. They might something like:

➜ "Oh come on, please join us"
➜ "Don't be like that, come with us"
➜ "We'd really like you to come"

Or it could be something much bigger or major! For example, your boss is being extremely rude and insulting. Perhaps yelling and screaming at the top of his or her lungs at you, making you really want to yell back and say something like:

➜ "How dare you speak to me that way!"
➜ "Shut-up!"
➜ "If you continue yelling at me, I'll walk out that door right now!"

Now I should point-out that to an interviewer, *conflict* and *problem* mean essentially the same thing. The only real difference between them is the word *conflict* generally refers to problems among people, such as personality clashes. *Problems* usually refer to everything else.

The important thing to remember is that having a conflict or problem is not good. They both must be dealt with quickly and properly. In other words, when you have a conflict, there's a "problem" that needs to be resolved. As a job seeker, you should consider them equal!

So when an interviewer asks how well you handle conflict, is the interviewer focusing on the smaller or in the larger problems? Now you might think the answer is simple, it's the bigger ones. Well you're partly correct. Yes, your answer should concentrate more on the serious conflicts that can arise. But you cannot ignore the little ones. Here is where many applicants make their mistake and drop the ball!

If left alone or mishandled, these smaller problems can very easily turn into larger ones. This is another part of what is being tested. Do you realize that failing to identify or resolve a problem sooner can often lead to bigger problems down the road? This is why it's so important for a candidate to show awareness and understanding of this concept. You need to explain that you would much rather deal with a conflict or problem sooner rather than later, because it's easier to resolve something smaller. An interviewer needs to hear you say it!

But is it always possible to identify or resolve things quickly and easily? Sometimes yes, but often times the answer is no. Why? Because you may not become aware of the problem until it's grown bigger. Or you may have thought it went away when it really didn't. Regardless, the interviewer needs to hear you are fully-prepared to handle the situation at any point!

The bottom-line is:

1. Conflicts are basically the same as problems because both aren't good and need to be resolved.
2. Explain your understanding that problems—both big and small—still need to be dealt with quickly. Otherwise, they can grow into even bigger problems. In other words, it's always better and easier to resolve something when it's smaller!
3. Discuss your overall strategy for dealing with conflicts and problems in general. This gives the interviewer a good sense of how you might handle a variety of problems that may arise on the job.
4. Feel free to *briefly* discuss an actual situation you had to highlight your problem-solving and conflict resolution skills in action. Briefly describe what the problem was, the steps you took to deal with it, and how things ultimately turned out.
5. Be prepared for an interviewer giving you various scenarios to test your ability to handle things. It's not uncommon to be given a situation or two to see how you might deal with them. You must show logical thinking, solid problem-solving, and a strong willingness to deal with the situation.

Tip: Resolving a problem or conflict doesn't necessarily mean it goes away completely. Sometimes, the most anyone can accomplish is that it's reduced enough to where everyone is satisfied. In other words, it may not be the ideal solution, but rather one that people can live with.

6. An interviewer will take this as a positive result. The reason why is because it's less of a problem now. That means your actions got some positive results! So any improvement is desirable and welcomed.

How Long You'd Stay

This particular question seems to catch many job seekers by surprise. Mainly because it's assumed they'll stick around for a while. But there are lots of people who will only stay until something better comes along. This is something employers realize and so the question is a test of whether a candidate is looking for a job or a career.

A candidate's willingness to remain longer tends to indicate a desire or willingness to grow along with the company. This is something that impresses an interviewer! But do bear in mind that an interviewer will take a close look at a candidate's work history to see how long that person has remained in his or her previous jobs. Why do they zero in on this? Well because it may indicate a pattern of job-hopping or bouncing around.

Someone who bounces around from job to job sends the message he or she will continue doing this. The interviewer may begin to think, "Why should we spend money to hire and train you if you're just going to move onto something else, just like you've done before?" Now here's something you may or may not know. It can sometimes cost tens of thousands of dollars to train a new employee! So interviewers tend to be more selective when it comes to deciding whom to consider for employment. Why? Because they don't look at you as someone just looking for work, but rather as an investment! An investment in time, resources, and money.

KEY: Willingness to join, learn, and grow!

In order to successfully handle this interview question, you must come across as someone who won't plan on leaving just because something better happens to come along. You need to show that you're looking for a "home." This means a place where you can use your talents, learn more, and grow as a person and as an employee. In other words, you're taking the same attitude as the employer—You are an investment!

They are selective and want to spend their money on a worthwhile investment. You are equally selective in terms of with whom you want to spend your working life. This is exactly why you're not merely jumping at whatever comes your way. An attitude like this will make an interviewer more likely to believe you plan on staying longer. Exactly how long that will be isn't known right now But you're already letting the interviewer know it's "longer." Long enough for you to be considered a worthwhile investment.

But you're not making any guarantees here either. Nobody knows exactly how long he or she will stay because anything can happen along the way. You're only saying that your plan right now is to find a place where you can fit-in nicely and grow. This is what the interviewer needs to hear and believe.

But suppose you're only looking for a job and not a career? For example, you're a teenager looking for summer work doing whatever and wherever as long as it pays. Do you want to lie to an employer by letting the interviewer know you want to make a career out of it? Of course not because that could devastate your chances. What you want to do here this is show you're still a good business investment. True, you don't plan on making a career out of it. But you also don't plan on just up and leaving tomorrow.

The point is that an interviewer always needs to be convinced you're worth their time, money, and resources. They're not stupid and do realize not everyone isn't looking for a career. All they really want is a pretty good sense that you'll remain "long enough." Once again, long enough for them to feel they got their monies worth.

The bottom-line is:

1. Always remember that it costs companies money, and takes both time and resources to hire and train you. So the inherent attitude of employers is, "Why should I spend all of this on you?"
2. Let the interviewer see your willingness and desire to learn from and grow with their company.
3. Show the interviewer you're a wise business investment by coming across as someone looking for a career, instead of a job. This way, you'll appear more likely to remain longer. In other words, you're playing into the notion that career-minded individuals will stay longer than those merely seeking a job (plain old work).

Tip: Regardless of whether or not you plan on making a career out of this, give the interviewer the sense you plan on staying "long enough." Long enough to justify their investment in time, money, and resources. Without this sense, your chances for success are greatly diminished!

What Would You Do Day 1?

Here's another good question for a candidate to be asked. What the interviewer is testing this time is your planning, organizing, and human relation skills. In other words, the interviewer wants to get a sense of whether you've actually given thought to your getting this job. If you have, how you might behave on your first day. After all, you are interviewing right? So isn't it reasonable to think about being offered the job? Yes, and that's exactly what the test is!

It's also a test of one's business sense. For example:

→ Will you walk in like gangbusters? Acting as though you already know everything and/or are in-charge.
→ Will you constantly raise how you did things at your previous job(s)?
→ Will you show openness to learning their way of doing things and/or learning new stuff?
→ Will you take notes?
→ Will you introduce yourself to others? Or will you wait for others to introduce themselves to you?
→ Will you look at how your desk is arranged? See what documents are on the computer, where stuff is, etc.

The keys here are to show the interviewer that you would:

→ Walk-in ready to learn this company's way of doing things.
→ Be ever-mindful that things may be done differently from what you're used to. Your first day isn't about explaining how you did things in the past or making tons of suggestions. It's about getting settled and learning how this company operates! You need to show an awareness of this.
→ Take detailed notes so you don't forget things.

Tip #1: Bring a pad and paper with you on your first day to show you're prepared to learn and write important things down. This makes you look very good!

→ Get the lay of the land to see where things are located, who's who, and how your work area is organized. This shows professionalism and a strong desire to get up and running right away!
→ Be ready to jump right in and work hard. In other words, although you may have a more relaxing first day because you don't know a lot yet, you are showing the interviewer your willingness to put in a full day's worth of work!
→ Be prepared to ask for help when needed so you won't mess-up and make mistakes. Mistakes that may very easily have been avoided if only you had asked for help.

The bottom-line is that you'll be:

1. At work and on-time. This is the most important because it forms the first impression of you on the job. There is no excuse for being late!

2. I've heard new employees say they had gotten lost on the way. The attitude of superiors in response to this was usually, "Well if you were smart, you would have taken a dry run first or planned ahead." In other words, you would have driven there to gauge traffic and make sure you know the way. And you would have adjusted for weather conditions and possible delays, such as getting lost. The point is you want to be there right on time.

Tip #2: When in doubt, always leave extra time

3. Pleasant and not come on strong with others. This means that you'll try your best to blend-in with others and be accepted by all.

4. Hard-working by putting in a full day's worth of work. In other words, you won't start your first day with the attitude of "It's going to be easy so I don't have to work hard today." You'll begin with the attitude of "I'm ready to work!"

5. Organized and prepared to begin your first day. This means you'll bring whatever they need from you to complete your new employee paperwork. For example, your Driver License and Social Security Card to complete your I-9 and W-2 forms.

6. Ready and willing to learn. In other words, you won't get upset if things are done differently. Instead, you'll be perfectly willing to adjust.

7. Open to advice and constructive criticism. You'll be glad to hear any suggestions on how to behave or do things so you won't make mistakes. But if you do, you'll correct them and learn not to do them again.

8. Willing to seek help wherever and whenever needed. This means you won't be afraid to ask others for help. Many new employees are afraid to do this because they feel it'll make them look bad. Especially when it's your very first day on the job.

9. But in reality, asking for help is a good thing! It's always better to admit you don't know what to do rather than giving it a try and then making a mistake. Not asking for help at first also opens the door to the attitude of "If you didn't know or were unsure, why didn't you just ask?"

10. Taking written notes so you won't forget important things. Many new employees don't do this and it's a *big* mistake! Why is taking notes the right thing to do? Because during your probationary period, which is usually 90 days, the employer is evaluating your performance to make sure they hired the right person.

11. Employers tend to remember approximately how many times you've asked the same question(s). In fact, I know of several people who've lost their jobs when the boss or trainer began to question if those people could handle the job. This was because, over and over again, they kept asking about things they were already taught and should have remembered.

12. I've also had students who thought they'll automatically be given a training manual containing everything they'll need to know. Sometimes yes, but most often no! Most employee manuals

give you the important things, but not everything. And some don't even give you an employee manual, but rather explain things verbally.

13. By writing things down, you're not only showing professionalism, but also have something to refer back to when needed. You can also put things into your own words so you'll understand it. And you'll really impress an employer because not everyone will do this. So you'll standout in a very good way!

Working Alone or in Groups

The question of whether you prefer working alone or in groups (teams) tests three things:

1. Your personality or temperament
2. Your interpersonal relations
3. Your ability to work under different environments.

To be successful here, you need to address and pass all three of these tests. So how do you do this? Let's begin with the personality test. The interviewer is deciding if you like being around people. Generally-speaking, someone who prefers working in a group tends to enjoy the company of others more. In other words, he or she prefers more "people contact." In addition, this type of person tends to be more outgoing. He or she will often be more willing to begin and join in conversations, speak-up, and participate in activities.

By contrast, someone who prefers working more independently or alone will tend to be the exact opposite. This type of person isn't as much of a "people-person." He or she will tend to be less outgoing, less willing to begin or join in conversations, and less likely to participate in activities and speak-up.

Notice how I don't say that someone who prefers working in groups *is* this or that. Nor do I do that for someone who prefers working more alone. Why? Because each person is different and these are merely general tendencies, not absolutes. Interviewers understand this, which is why being one way or the other isn't an automatic disqualification. But they do take these tendencies into consideration when determining if you'd be a good fit for the job.

Here's a side-by-side comparison of the two personality types. It gives you some typical characteristics associated with each. On the left, we have someone who prefers working more alone. On the right, we have the one who prefers working more in group settings. Once again, these are general tendencies, not absolutes. I strongly suggest taking a good look at this to decide which category best describes you. The reason is because that's exactly what an interviewer is going to do! Or better yet, ask someone else who knows you well to do this and see if there's agreement. As I mentioned earlier in this book, others may see us differently than we see ourselves. So getting another's perspective can be quite useful when preparing for interviews.

Personality Comparison

Working Alone	Working in Groups
➲ Introverted	➲ Extraverted
➲ Less outgoing	➲ More outgoing
➲ Soft-spoken and less likely to speak-up	➲ Outspoken and more likely to speak-up
➲ Prefers stability and routine	➲ Flexible and open to change
➲ Remains in same job longer	➲ Changes jobs and/or moves-up
➲ Detail-oriented	➲ Less detailed-oriented
➲ Follower	➲ Leader
▪ Takes orders	▪ Gives orders
▪ Follows decisions	▪ Makes decisions
▪ Less likely to take charge	▪ Takes charge
▪ Less likely to show initiative	▪ Shows initiative

KEY #1: Make sure your personality fits the job and/or profession.

You need to show the interviewer that you've got the right personality for this position. Let's see if you can tell which type of person may be better-suited for these jobs and fields. In other words, I'm putting you in the role of an interviewer and your job is to determine which personality you think would be the "right fit." I think you'll find this exercise to be rather helpful and useful.

Exercise: What type of personality does this job require?

Job	Personality Type	
1. Customer Service	☐ Alone	☐ Group
2. Bookkeeper	☐ Alone	☐ Group
3. Sales	☐ Alone	☐ Group
4. Computer Programmer	☐ Alone	☐ Group
5. Retail Sales Clerk	☐ Alone	☐ Group
6. File Clerk	☐ Alone	☐ Group
7. Call Center or Telemarketer	☐ Alone	☐ Group
8. Forklift Driver	☐ Alone	☐ Group
9. Receptionist	☐ Alone	☐ Group
10. Nurse	☐ Alone	☐ Group

By doing this exercise, I think you've learned that it requires knowing something about these jobs and fields. In other words, if you don't know what a Telemarketer does, then how can you tell which personality is needed? So it's very important to know as much as possible about your particular field and the various jobs within it. This way, you'll be in a much better position to explain how your personality matches it. So what are the correct answers? For that, you'll need to turn to the end of this chapter.

Let's now move on to the second test, which is on your interpersonal skills. The interviewer is now focusing on how well you can interact with others. He or she is asking the question "How well can you relate to these two personality types? In other words, the interviewer want to see if you can get along and work well with them.

KEY #2: Be able to relate "well-enough" to *both* personalities!

Regardless of whether you'll be working mostly or exclusively with one type or the other, you still need to be able to interact with both. The reasons are because people change jobs, get promoted, move between departments, etc. An interviewer looks for someone who can handle these because they'll tend to stay longer. He or she would rather hire someone who's capable of effectively interacting with both personality types. That's because you never know where you'll be in the future. So interviewers prefer to hire someone who can grow and develop. The candidate who shows a strong ability to interact well with both personalities "fits the bill."

Now let's move on to our third and final test, which is your ability to perform in either environment. Here the focus is on your job performance. The second test focused on your interacting with others to see if you can just get along. But here, it's on whether you will be able to do good work when working alongside or with these people.

KEY #3: Be able to perform well when surrounded by both types.

You need to show an interviewer that no matter with whom you'll be working, you can get along just fine and do great work. You may prefer one type over the other. But you're letting the interviewer know that you can get along and work with people having either personality. So personality type isn't really a factor.

The bottom-line is:

1. Match your personality type to what's needed. This is where knowing more about the profession and the job can be extremely helpful. In other words, make sure the interviewer feels your personality matches the job *and* the profession. This way, it'll look like we have a good match!
2. Show that you can get along with literally anyone and still do a good job. In other words, your having a different personality than someone else won't effect your ability to get along and do good work.

Earlier in this chapter, I had given you an exercise to put you in the role of an interviewer. Your task was to look at each of the jobs and professions in the table below, and decide which type of personality you felt would be better.

Here are the solutions and the reasons why so you'll understand how an interviewer thinks.

Exercise: What type of personality does this job require?

Job	Personality Type	
1. Customer Service	☐ Alone	■ Group
2. Bookkeeper	■ Alone	☐ Group
3. Sales	☐ Alone	■ Group
4. Computer Programmer	■ Alone	☐ Group
5. Retail Sales Clerk	☐ Alone	■ Group
6. File Clerk	■ Alone	☐ Group
7. Call Center or Telemarketer	☐ Alone	■ Group
8. Forklift Driver	■ Alone	☐ Group
9. Receptionist	☐ Alone	■ Group
10. Nurse	☐ Alone	■ Group

The ultimate key to getting this exercise right, lies in knowing whether or not there is a lot of contact with people.

➔ If the answer is *yes*, then it would tend to require someone who prefers working more in groups.
➔ If the answer is *no*, then it would tend to require someone who prefers working more independently or alone.

With customer service, it's pretty obvious that you're providing service to people ("customers"). The same goes for a Nurse. He or she would be working very closely with patients, who would be considered the "customers." In sales, whether it's retail, financial, insurance, etc, you're still working closely with customers. Successful salespeople know how important developing good relations with their customers is. So there's tremendous contact with people. Those who work in telemarketing or in a call center are basically doing sales. The only difference is they're talking to customers mainly over the phone rather than in-person. A Receptionist is the first person you see when you walk into an office, so contact with people is a big part of the job. He or she will greet people as they come in, talk to them on the phone, and interact with others in the office.

So all of these jobs would tend to require someone who prefers working more in a group. Why? Because the personality this person would have is generally more "people-oriented." He or she tends to be more outgoing, more comfortable around and interacting with people, and a better communicator.

Bookkeepers record financial transactions, such as today's sales. They may also prepare some financial reports. Do you think this person could enter things without mistakes if they were interrupted with phone calls and/or people walking-up to them? Of course not! Computer programmers basically sit in front of a computer and type lines and lines of code. Some work on an entire software program, while others work on just their individual piece of a larger program. Do you think they could do this accurately and speedy if they were interrupted? No! File Clerks make, copy, retrieve, and put away files. Think they could misfile something if they get interrupted? Yes! Forklift drivers stack and retrieve stuff for most of their day. They'll tend to work in areas where customers aren't permitted and so contact with people is more limited.

So each of these jobs would tend to need somebody who's more comfortable working more independently and alone. Someone who doesn't mind having a daily routine that rarely changes. In other words, someone who enjoys doing the same thing over and over again.

Why This Profession or Field?

This question is a really good one to see if a candidate has done his or her homework. In other words, it tests your researching ability and personality. The interviewer wants to know exactly what it is about this profession that makes you want to be a part of it. The interview will then decide if he or she feels you are cutout if for it.

The more you know about different fields and the various jobs within them, the better you'll do here. It's because the interviewer wants *specifics*, meaning details! You need to demonstrate full knowledge of what the profession is all about. Then you need to match yourself to it. In other words, you must show the interviewer that you are cutout for the field and would do well working in it.

KEY #1: Know what *this* profession and job itself involves

KEY #2: Understand what type of person would be successful in this field and job

KEY #3: Show how *you* are a good fit for this profession and job

Let's use someone who wants to work as a Medical Assistant as an example. An interviewer needs to know you have a clear understanding of the major tasks you'll most likely have to do on the job. But knowing more is always better. Job descriptions tend to list the major tasks and so there isn't much research involved. But walking into your interview knowing beyond this shows you actually took the time to investigate and research things further. That makes you look even better because you made the effort to learn more and do some research. It might also be just enough to standout from your competition and improve your chances of success!

So what exactly does a Medical Assistant do? Generally-speaking, he or she would:

➔ Greet patients when they walk into the office
➔ Schedule appointments, tests, and follow-ups
➔ Create and maintain patient records
➔ Handle billing and insurance
➔ Take patient vitals, such as: height, weight, and blood pressure

The job description might just say, "Take vitals," without going into more detail. But if you walk in knowing some vitals you'll probably be taking, you're showing a knowledge of the profession and job. This highlights your knowledge, training, and researching. Something that will make you look very good to an interviewer!

But most important is to show you have a clear understanding of the profession as a whole. In other words, having a knowledge of:

→ The type of personality this field or job would tend to require
→ The necessary and desirable skills, experience, and training
→ The various jobs within this profession
→ Other jobs or fields that are or may be related

To be successful in the medical profession, you may need some formal training in things like basic terminology or insurance coding. You'd also have to enjoy medicine and working closely with patients. In addition, you'd need solid organizational and time-management skills. If you plan on working in a bigger office with a very large number of patients and/or multiple physicians, then you'd have to be able to cope with a potentially stressful and hectic work environment. You'd also need to relate well to patients having a variety of problems. Depending on the severity of the problem, it may be pretty tough to handle emotionally. For instance, you can *never* appear disgusted or horrified! Doing so may humiliate, upset, or make the patient feel bad. Your job is to make patients feel more at ease and comfortable.

An interviewer needs to see you understand all of this. He or she also needs to see that you have the right personality. Someone who's more cold and distant by nature wouldn't fit-in well in this environment. It requires someone who can empathize with the patients and make them feel welcomed. Not someone who will shun or be disgusted by them. If you have the training, education, and perhaps experience needed, then say so! But if you lack any or all of these, then show a willingness to learn and do whatever it takes. Why? Because it's what you want to do. And you want to succeed!

The bottom-line is:

1. Make sure you show a great deal of enthusiasm. Doing this sends the message you really want to be a part of that profession and succeed.
2. Show confidence in your ability to do well it in this profession and job!
3. Research the field and it's various jobs. Learn what personality, skills, and training are needed. Look at other job descriptions to discover what the various job duties may be.
4. Match yourself to all this! Show the interviewer how you're a very good fit for this profession. Be specific as to why you feel this way.

All Right to Run a Credit Check?

According to the Equal Employment Opportunity Commission (EEOC), an employer cannot refuse to hire someone with poor or bad credit. That is unless there's a "reasonable" explanation. Most job seekers aren't aware of this and so they are totally unprepared for a question like this.

An interviewer is looking to protect the company. Protect it from someone who may steal things or commit some other crime. For example, you're interviewing for a job as a Cashier. Does an employer want someone handling cash who isn't trustworthy and responsible? No. The same thing goes for someone applying for a job as a Bank Teller where you're surrounded by lots of cash. Or a Jeweler who's surrounded by rare or precious stones. But what does your credit rating or report have to do with jobs like these?

Someone with poor credit may be more tempted to steal in order to repay those to whom they owe money. The ones who are owed the money are called *creditors*. This is a perfectly legitimate concern to an employer. The real question is whether having bad credit automatically means you will steal. No! But you may be more *tempted* by it. That's a risk many employers just don't want to run. So obtaining a credit report can be considered all right and legitimate in these cases.

> **Tip #1**: You must be told they're going to run a credit check. In other words, you'll be asked to sign an authorization form.

Now if your credit is good, then there's really no problem. You know your report will come back clean and you'll appear trustworthy and responsible. What if you don't trust the employer to protect your personal and financial information? Well if that's the case, then why would you want to work for them?

After all, you'll be giving them lots of personal information. Information like your Social Security Number, date of birth, etc. And if your pay will be made by direct deposit, then they'll need your bank name and account number. But suppose your credit isn't so good or you're not sure? The issue then becomes, do you:

- Allow it and explain my situation to the interviewer right now?
- Allow it and wait until the report comes back to explain my situation?
- Simply refuse and move on to another company?
- Say absolutely nothing and hope they won't find out?

> **KEY**: Show honesty!

The simple fact is many people have gotten themselves into financial trouble and so you're not alone. We're literally bombarded day in and day out with credit card offers. Those already in financial trouble, and can least afford it, tend to get them the most! That's because the credit card companies can make more money by collecting late fees and charging higher interest. In other words, those with bad credit often provide more revenue than those with good credit. That's because those with poorer credit tend to pay late or make the minimum payment. People with good credit generally pay their bills on-time and in full. So it's more profitable to the credit card companies to have people with poorer credit.

My point is that an interviewer will respect and admire your having the guts to admit you made a financial mistake and dug yourself into a financial hole. Why? Because you're taking full responsibility for your actions and mistake! The most important thing is to explain how you are dealing with it. In other words, you want to *reassure* the interviewer you're handling the situation. This way, you're letting him or her know that you don't need to steal. In other words, you already have the situation under control and don't need their money to repay creditors. It's the attitude of "I made a mistake in the past, paid a heavy price, learned from it, and won't repeat it again!"

Besides, having poor credit is just another problem. And problems need to be resolved. So admitting you have a problem, and then explaining how you resolved it, highlights your strong problem-solving abilities. In the workplace, effective problem-solving is a very good thing. So is honesty and taking responsibility for your actions. With my strategy, you'll be demonstrating all three of these positive and important workplace attitudes! That makes you far more impressive and improves your chances of success.

The bottom-line is:

1. Allow the employer to run their credit check regardless of whether or not your credit is good.
2. It doesn't matter if you feel a credit check is needed. What's important is the employer feels it's necessary!

Tip #2: Jobs involving the handling of cash or other valuables will quite often require credit checks as part of the hiring process. The same is true for jobs needing security clearance or in the public sector (government jobs).

3. If your credit is good, then you have nothing to fear. You can trust employers to protect your information and keep it confidential. If you didn't trust them, then you wouldn't want to work there.
4. If your credit is poor, I suggest being open and honest about it. Reassure the interviewer that you're dealing with it and don't need to steal from them because it's under control. In other words, you made a financial mistake in the past, have learned from it, and are taking full responsibility! This showcases your problem-solving ability making you much better to the interviewer.

How You Effectively Communicate

This question tests your communication skills. The interviewer is looking to see whether you know the best way to communicate under different situations. For example:

➔ When is sending an e-mail better?
➔ When is it better to explain something verbally?
➔ When should it be written down on paper?"

The interviewer is determining if you even know what effective communication is. Communication is simply the conveying the information. But *effective* communication means doing this in a manner where the information is completely understood. And the format used is appropriate for the situation. In other words, it's not the words that are used, but also your format, tone, and style. Suppose I were to write a letter to a customer that included the following:

Please sign and return the documents using the enclosed SASE.

Is there anything wrong with the way I wrote this? Well that all depends on whether you know what "SASE" means. Maybe you do, but then again, perhaps not. *SASE* is an acronym for Self-Addressed Stamped Envelope. My point is that the reader may or may not understand this abbreviation. If he or she doesn't, then I didn't effectively communicate my instructions.

Remember, effective communication is when your meaning is crystal clear. So a more effective way to have written the letter would be something like:

Please sign the enclosed documents where indicated. Upon completion, return them to us in the provided return envelope.

By rewriting the original sentence, I have:

1. Avoided using an abbreviation that may or may not be understood by the reader
2. Used plain and simple wording that's more easily understood by all
3. Communicated the proper meaning
4. Worded it in a highly professional and business-like manner

Now the one area today where we tend to abbreviate and throw grammar and spelling out the window is with e-mail. That's because many people take the attitude of "Who cares if there are spelling or grammatical errors? All that matters is they understand what I mean."

Well there are those around the world who do care! Business communication, whether it's verbal, on paper, in an e-mail, etc, is still a reflection of you and your company. Having a poorly written e-mail can reflect badly upon your business.

It could be taken as a sign you don't:

- ➜ Realize there are problems with it
- ➜ Care how it makes you look
- ➜ Know how to write
- ➜ Review and double-check things
- ➜ Worry about or concern yourself with small details

Do any of these make you look professional? No! But in an interview, it's super important to be seen as the consummate professional. In other words, you must demonstrate your ability to communicate well. After all, an interview is a form of communication. This means you are being judged on how well you communicate. *Effective* communication scores you big points!

Tip #1:   Bring something to highlight your solid communication skills

As I've said before, a great way to showcase your talents is to hand the interviewer something concrete that makes you look good. What works well here is a copy of something you've written that looks great. Or something that wasn't originally written very well that you've revised and improved. Both of these show the interviewer you are capable of writing effectively. And if you can do it on paper, then you can do it verbally or in an e-mail.

Tip #2:   Avoid or don't overuse technical jargon

When communicating, it's generally best to use simpler language instead of a bunch of technical words. This is an area where many helpdesk personnel and others working in technical fields struggle. It's often hard for the customers to explain their problems in more technical terms. It's sometimes equally hard for the techs to explain things in simpler terms. Matters can be further complicated if all this is being done over the telephone.

So how do you more effectively communicate with customers in these situations? Well you need to put yourself in their place and basically assume "They know nothing." In other words, look at it from the perspective of you're back in school re-learning the material for the first time. Think about how your teacher would explain it to you.

Tip #3:   Choose the right communication format

There are times when e-mail might work better. Other times, it may not be your best option. For example, when sending a thank you note after an interview. Some would simply write an e-mail to the interviewer. Now there's nothing wrong with this per se, but it's pretty cold and impersonal. Why? Because it doesn't take much effort on your part and it's just words on a computer screen.

But sending a note on paper is a different story. It's more than just words on a piece of paper. It's going that extra mile to write the note and sign it. Handwriting your note instead of typing it on the computer is even better. Why? Because it adds a more personal touch. Just make sure your handwritten note is readable!

Tip #4:   Writing more slowly can make your script look neater and more readable

Now suppose you were going to fire somebody. Would you just send that person an e-mail? Believe it or not, there are actually companies that do this! In fact, I had a student who knew someone at his company who got an e-mail firing notice. Does this seem like a nice way to fire somebody? No! Would a nicer way to terminate someone be to tell that person face-to-face? Yes.

I had a situation many years ago while working in a bank. One of our employees had grabbed his briefcase, smiled at everyone, and said he was going to lunch. About two or three hours later, I had asked if anybody saw him come back; nobody did. So I asked someone in the office who was friends with him if he had quit. The co-worker didn't have a clue. A few days later, we received a letter in the mail from him telling us that he quit. Was that smile his way of communicating his leaving? Who knows.

The point is that communication can also be non-verbal or non-written. For instance, body language is a form of communication. It's also a big part of what an interviewer concentrates on during your interview. That's because it can reveal a great deal about you. It helps determine if you are being sincere and honest with your words. That's why it's so important to look and act the part, not just speak it. You need to match your body language to your words and writing.

Tip #5:   Use appropriate tone and style

When we communicate, there are varying ways to say the same thing. Some are more straightforward; others are more roundabout. Your tone and style should be appropriate for the situation. If your goal is to convey a sense of creativity, then the tone and style should be more fun, exciting, and creative. If your objective is to convey professionalism, then your tone and style should be more formal and business-like.

For example, someone looking for work as an Illustrator or Designer may put his or her resume on stationary. Why? Because using a more fancy paper or background might convey the impression of somebody who's very creative. This same impression can also be accomplished by using a fancier font.

But for a person seeking employment as a Front Desk Clerk, doing these things would be inappropriate. Why? Because the image of a Front Desk Clerk is very different from that of an Illustrator or Designer. Somebody working at a front desk must demonstrate a high degree of professionalism, rather than creativity. Using a fancy font or paper would create the wrong impression. The impression you really want to convey is that of a true business professional. So you would behave more formal and business-like.

People working in certain areas of the medical field have to be very careful when it comes to their wording. If someone was seriously ill and didn't survive, would you just say to the family he or she died? No. You would tend to word it in a more somber and caring tone. Using something more along the lines of you're very sorry to inform them he or she has "passed away."

Funeral Directors also have to be careful with what they say, and how they say it. Can they smile when showing somebody the various caskets? No! Can they be all business and show no emotion? No! Can they speak in a louder or more booming voice? No! Communicating in these ways would be very inappropriate for the situation. They're dealing with the families of people who are deceased. This isn't a time for happiness and smiles! So Funeral Directors must adjust their tone of voice, choice of words and clothing, and body language accordingly.

This is also important for you to do when taking interviews. You must speak, write, and behave accordingly depending on the situation. If you are dealing with an angry customer, you don't want to raise your voice and yell back. Nor do you want to take a more aggressive posture. These are confrontational behaviors! Instead, you need to empathize with the customer and become an advocate for him or her. In other words, you need to appease the customer to make him or her feel you understand and are trying to help as best as you can. Well during an interview, you need to demonstrate this same awareness.

Tip #6:   Make certain words and/or points standout

The use of bold, italics, underline, numbering, or bullets in your written communication can be very powerful tools. They can be used to draw the reader's attention to certain things. You just need decide which of these would work best in your situation. You also need to take your audience and purpose into consideration before making your decision. But don't overuse them! The reason is because overuse tends to lessen the impact.

I'll give you a good example. A friend of mine works in Human Resources. She has to send letters to all employees letting each one know what his or her benefits are. Here are four possible ways those letters could be worded.

Version 1:

The benefits you currently have are: Regency Health Plan 1, 401(k), Providence Dental, and Accidental Death and Dismemberment.

Version 2:

The benefits you currently have are:
1. Regency Health Plan 1,
2. 401(k),
3. Providence Dental, and
4. Accidental Death and Dismemberment.

Version 3:

The benefits you currently have are:

> 1. *Regency Health Plan 1,*
> 2. *401(k),*
> 3. *Providence Dental, and*
> 4. *Accidental Death and Dismemberment.*

Version 4:

The benefits you currently have are: **Regency Health Plan 1**, **401(k)**, **Providence Dental**, *and* **Accidental Death and Dismemberment**.

Which of these four versions do you think works best? Now before you answer, let me say that there are no rights or wrongs here. Each of you is allowed to have your own opinion. But there are some legitimate reasons for choosing one version over another.

Let me point some of them out to you right now.

➔ In *version 1*, we have one long sentence stating each of the benefits this person has. But the problem is those benefits *blend-in* with the rest of the text. They just don't standout from the rest of the text!

➔ Contrast this with *version 4*, which is also one big sentence. Notice how each benefit is *bolded* to standout. See how it draws your attention to each one of them. But is there just too much bolding here? In my professional opinion, there is. That's because literally half the sentence is bolded. And bolded right next to each other. In other words, does your eye focus more on the bolded or the non-bolded text? Regardless of how you may feel, it's definitely an improvement over *version 1*!

➔ *Versions 2 and 3* are pretty similar. They both use *numbering* to separate-out each benefit. This way, the reader knows how many benefits he or she has, and what each one is. Since each benefit occupies it's own separate line, it doesn't run together as in *versions 1 and 4*.

➔ The main difference between *versions 2 and 3* is the positioning of the benefits. *Version 3* indents them to make them standout more clearly. The eye immediately catches the indent in version 3. So I would have to say that *version 3* would be your best choice.

The bottom-line is

1. Understand there is a difference between communication and effective communication. *Effective* communication means getting your point across very clearly by using an appropriate communication format, wording, tone, and style.
2. Have a good sense of which form of communication would work best in various situations.

3. Never forget that you and your business are reflected in your communications. So it's important to be sure anything communicated is done so in a highly professional manner!

4. E-mail should be written properly. In other words, view e-mail as you would a letter to a customer. Make it professional and project a positive image of yourself and your company.

5. Choose your words carefully based upon the situation. And understand that's it's better to use words that are more easily comprehended. This means avoiding or not overusing technical terms, lingo or jargon, and abbreviations.

Analytical Skills

There are basically two ways to ask this question. One is where the candidate is asked to describe his or her own analytical skills. The second is through scenarios. In other words, the interviewer gives you various situations where you need to apply some analytical thought or do some analysis. But regardless of how the question is structured, the interviewer wants to test your ability to use logical thought.

A very common mistake by job seekers is to assume that analytical skills only refer to one's ability to crunch numbers. But in reality, analytical skills refer to the notions of logical thought and reasoning. This can apply to both number-crunching and beyond. Let me give you a perfect example.

Some people will refer to a Psychiatrist or Psychologist as an Analyst. Does this automatically mean he or she analyzes numbers? No. It simply means that he or she analyzes the patient. Numbers aren't being crunched, but rather an assessment of what's going on inside the patient's mind is being conducted.

So regardless of whether or not the analysis involves number-crunching, the key lies in the use of logical thought. You must carefully assess things in order to make judgments and draw conclusions. This is what the interviewer is really after! He or she wants to see that you have the capacity to gather information, weigh alternatives, and draw your own conclusions.

KEY #1:   Analytical thinking means being methodical and logical

When discussing your ability to analyze, it's important to show that you understand it's a process. A process that involves the gathering and interpreting of information. It may also require getting other points of view to help draw the right conclusion. In addition, it may involve comparing things to an established standard or benchmark.

In other words, it involves going from point A to B to C to D, etc. You can't skip over B and go straight to D. So it's important to show the interviewer that you know how to progress from one step to the next.

KEY #2:   Conclusions aren't always right

Even with the proper analysis, a conclusion may not be correct. This is because there are many instances when conclusions are personal judgments. In other words, the facts could support multiple conclusions. Which one is the "right one" is a matter of personal opinion. An interviewer wants to see if you understand this. Whatever conclusion(s) you ultimately reach, there must be solid and sound reasoning backing it!

The bottom-line is:

1.   Analysis is the process of gathering and interpreting information.

2. Analysis means using logical thought and sound reasoning to make judgments and/or draw conclusions.
3. Analysis may or may not involve working with numbers.
4. Good analysis may still lead to multiple conclusions that are open to opinion.
5. Good analysis means your information must be current, timely, relevant, and trusted or reliable. Otherwise, your conclusions may be wrong!
6. And in the workplace, a wrong or invalid conclusion can cause trouble or cost you money. For example, getting someone into trouble or loosing out on a sale. Or failing to take advantage of a money-making ideal or strategy.

Handling Deadlines

The question of how you deal with or handle deadlines tests four things, your:

1.   Organizational skills
2.   Time-management ability
3.   Problem-solving skills
4.   Ability to handle stress and pressure

Deadlines are sometimes known in advance. But other times, they suddenly appear or change at the last minute. An interviewer needs to see you realize all of this. But most important is that you can effectively deal with them!

> **KEY #1**:   Prioritize and organize!

Effective time-management requires a strong ability to organize and rank tasks in order of importance. This way, the highest priority ones get the most attention. And more importantly, get completed on-time and done right. But you cannot ignore the lower priority tasks! They must also get enough attention. And depending upon who you work for, you may have to contend with a boss who sees everything he or she gives you as being top priority.

So part of effective prioritizing and organization involves your determining what's really important and should get the most attention, and what should not. In addition, you may have to deal with an older and less important task suddenly becoming more important. All this requires your making constant adjustments on the job as new tasks are added and older ones are completed. You need to show an interviewer that you can do this.

> **Tip**:   If you work for or support multiple people, you'll need to organize and prioritize each person's individual work. You'll also need to manage your own time so everyone feels he or she is getting enough attention.

This requires a strong ability to multitask. And realizing that the more people you work for, the greater your workload can be. So there's often a direct relationship between your workload and the number of people you support or work for.

More people = increased workload and pressure!

However, you might work for one person who loads you up with tons of work. So you must be able to handle both situations! In other words, regardless of how many people you work for, you need to be able to prioritize, organize, and get things done!

KEY #2: Deadlines can often lead to increased stress and pressure

It's common for employees to feel more stress as a deadline grows closer or changes. They begin to wonder if:

➜ The deadline will be met
➜ Work quality will be good enough
➜ The boss will be happy or satisfied with the results
➜ Instructions were followed
➜ The formatting will look nice

You need to show an awareness of this. But you also need to demonstrate your ability to deal with this pressure. In other words, pressure and deadlines simply go together! And an effective worker handles it well and gets the job done.

KEY #3: Problems may arise at anytime and must be dealt with

As I mentioned earlier, it's possible that a deadline could change and be moved up. That's a problem for you to handle. In other words, you now have to rearrange things and deal with the earlier timeframe. How you'd adjust and handle the situation is part of what an interviewer is testing. You may also have a problem if you need information from an outside source or another employee.

For example, in order to put your report together, you need some information from another department. Let's assume you told them you needed that info by the end of the week. Well they dragged their feet because it wasn't a major priority to them and missed the deadline. Because of that, you're unable to get your report completed. So you've got a problem that needs to be resolved.

Another common problem is constantly being interrupted while working on something important. Maybe your boss is always asking you how it's coming. Perhaps the phone is ringing off the hook and taking you away from your tasks. Or people are walking up to your desk with questions or more work. And maybe your coworkers are just coming over to chit-chat with you at the wrong time. It's important you demonstrate solid problem-solving skills here. And understand that problems can arise at any moment and must be dealt with promptly and correctly.

The bottom-line is:

1. Deadlines are just a normal part of any job. In other words, it goes with the territory.
2. Deadlines, stress, and pressure go together. The interviewer needs to know you understand this and can handle them.

3. Not all deadlines can be met! You may not have enough time to get the job finished, or done to your boss' satisfaction. It's possible your boss may set an arbitrary deadline or hit you at the last minute with something important.

4. Again, this just goes with the territory and shouldn't phase you. Being a true professional means you realize this and will deal with it the best you can. And that's the most anybody can do!

5. Supporting or working for more people means multiple deadlines and greater demands on your time. Some of which may conflict. In other words, you may have two people with the same deadline. Maybe you can get both jobs done. But then again, maybe not. You'll need to show your professionalism by explaining how you'd manage or handle this situation.

6. You do this by showing how you'd prioritize things and allocate your time. This way, you're demonstrating your ability to effectively multitask. And you'll be sure everyone you support or report to feels they are getting a fair amount of your time. In other words, you'll make sure they aren't feeling ignored or are never a priority.

Why Leave Your Job?

It's very common for an interviewer to ask a candidate why he or she is leaving or has left a particular job. So the question is pretty straightforward in that sense. The question can also be worded in a number of ways. For example:

→ Why did you leave your last or most recent job?
→ Tell me why you plan on leaving your current job?
→ Why do you want to leave your present job?
→ Why did you leave _____ job? In this case, the interviewer is asking why you left a specific job listed your resume or application.

Regardless of how the question is asked, the interviewer's main focus is on two things. The first is an attempt to discover your true reason(s) for leaving or wanting to leave. The second is to see whether you'll speak negatively about your current or former employer. A common mistake by applicants is to say very negative things about their current or previous employer(s). In other words, the candidate will be brutally honest. For example:

→ My boss is a total incompetent or an SOB
→ My boss is dumb and makes lots of bad or stupid decisions
→ Company policies are ridiculous or stupid
→ I hated that company
→ The company's run badly

Saying these sorts of things is badmouthing and doesn't make you look good. So it's extremely important that you never do this! An interviewer may begin to wonder if *you* are the one with the problem. The interviewer might also wonder if you'll say things like this about his or her company.

Instead, you should focus your answer on reasons that will sound more positive and business-like. This means giving the interviewer reasons that are perfectly understandable and legitimate. Reasons that make you look like a true professional who uses sound business reasoning and judgment.

Here are some acceptable and legitimate reasons for leaving your job:

→ Little or no room for growth or advancement. This means you've gone as far as you can in that company or office

➜ Aspects of the job you previously enjoyed have been taken away, reduced, or minimized. So what you enjoyed most is no longer the main part of your job. This makes your job more boring, less enjoyable, or less challenging

➜ The company or industry is going through some very rough times. For example, layoffs or downsizing. You want to move into something more stable where you don't have to worry about this

➜ You want something more closely related to your schooling. This says you're not looking for a job, but rather a career

➜ The company is very large and you would prefer working in a smaller or more family environment. In other words, you're tired of being viewed as "employee number ..."

Whatever you say, it has to be something more positive. Something to which the interview can relate and say, "I can understand why you want to leave." Now sometimes, this isn't easy. Especially if you feel you're being forced-out. And in cases where you're constantly being criticized or yelled at. Or if you work for a very nasty or abusive boss who disrespects you.

But you must rise above this and be the consummate professional! Don't stoop to their level by becoming nasty yourself. You must bite the bullet and provide more business-like and legitimate reasons for wanting out. Besides, it's quite possible the interviewer knows and happens to like your boss. So being negative about him or her only serves to makes you look bad. But basing your decision on more sound and legitimate reasons makes you look good!

The bottom-line is:

1. *Never* roast or badmouth your current or previous employers. Always be the consummate professional and project a positive image!
2. Remember that it's quite possible the interviewer may know and like your boss or company.
3. Give valid and understandable reason(s) for wanting to leave.

Questions for the interviewer?

When an interviewer asks if you have any questions, that's a clear indication your interview is nearing conclusion. Now a classic interview mistake is for a candidate to say he or she has no questions. It's a mistake because it signals one of two things:

1. All your questions have already been answered
2. You can't think of any to ask

An interviewer is testing your understanding that's it's impossible to answer every conceivable question in such a short period of time. In other words, because an interview is relatively short, there have to be questions for the interviewer.

KEY: Always ask the interviewer a question!

To be successful, you must ask the interviewer at least a question or two. Now depending upon how your interview goes, there may be some obvious unanswered questions to ask. For example, if the interviewer did not discuss the working conditions, you could ask about it. But what if the interviewer seemingly answered all your questions? Or you get nervous and cannot think of anything. Here's a helpful strategy you can use in these situations:

Tip: When you're unable to think of any questions, ask for a clarification or verification of something that's already been said.

In other words, repeat something the interviewer had already mentioned and say you just want to verify or reiterate it. This way, you're letting the interviewer know you were paying attention and want to double-check your facts before you leave. Some important questions you may want to ask are:

➔ Can you describe a typical day?

Asking an interviewer to describe a typical day on the job can be extremely revealing. You will gain an excellent sense of what the job will actually be like and involve. This may also expose some hidden pressures or problems you could face if you accept the job. So I personally think this is a great question to ask.

➔ Could you tell me about the working conditions?

This can tell you a lot about the pressures or problems you could face. For example, you might discover that the job involves a lot of running around the office, instead of just sitting at your desk for most of the day. It's often the little things we discover that can make the difference between our enjoying the job and hating it.

➔ What happened to the last person who had this job?

This may seem like a rather odd question to ask, but I feel it's a very good one. For instance, if the interviewer says that he or she was promoted, then you know the company promotes from within. If the interviewer tells you that he or she didn't work out, then you know they want somebody highly-qualified who stands a good chance of working out this time around. But if the interviewer avoids or dances around the question, then that could indicate something bad happened. In other words, the answer to this question could tell you if you're going from the frying pan into the fire.

Here are some more questions you may want to ask:

➔ Is there an opportunity to grow or move-up? And if so, to what?
➔ What benefits do you offer? Medical? Dental? Vision? 401(k)?
➔ Who will be the one training me?
➔ How long will my training last?

The bottom-line is:

1. *Never* end your interview without asking at least a question or two! Interviews are relatively short and there's always more to know.
2. If you can't think of any questions, then ask the interviewer to confirm or clarify something that was previously said. This way, you're simply double-checking things before you leave.
3. Don't dwell on salary or benefits. You don't want the interviewer to get the sense you're more interested in the money and perks than the job itself. You want the interviewer to see that you enjoy the profession and want a job that's right for you. In other words, job satisfaction is most important; salary and benefits are secondary.

This can tell you a lot about the pressures or problems you could face. For example, you might discover that the job involves a lot of running around the office, instead of just sitting at your desk for most of the day. It's often the little things we discover that can make the difference between our enjoying the job and hating it.

➔   What happened to the last person who had this job?

This may seem like a rather odd question to ask, but I feel it's a very good one. For instance, if the interviewer says that he or she was promoted, then you know the company promotes from within. If the interviewer tells you that he or she didn't work out, then you know they want somebody highly-qualified who stands a good chance of working out this time around. But if the interviewer avoids or dances around the question, then that could indicate something bad happened. In other words, the answer to this question could tell you if you're going from the frying pan into the fire.

Here are some more questions you may want to ask:

➔   Is there an opportunity to grow or move-up? And if so, to what?
➔   What benefits do you offer? Medical? Dental? Vision? 401(k)?
➔   Who will be the one training me?
➔   How long will my training last?

The bottom-line is:

1.   *Never* end your interview without asking at least a question or two! Interviews are relatively short and there's always more to know.
2.   If you can't think of any questions, then ask the interviewer to confirm or clarify something that was previously said. This way, you're simply double-checking things before you leave.
3.   Don't dwell on salary or benefits. You don't want the interviewer to get the sense you're more interested in the money and perks than the job itself. You want the interviewer to see that you enjoy the profession and want a job that's right for you. In other words, job satisfaction is most important; salary and benefits are secondary.

This can tell you a lot about the pressures or problems you could face. For example, you might discover that the job involves a lot of running around the office, instead of just sitting at your desk for most of the day. It's often the little things we discover that can make the difference between our enjoying the job and hating it.

→ What happened to the last person who had this job?

This may seem like a rather odd question to ask, but I feel it's a very good one. For instance, if the interviewer says that he or she was promoted, then you know the company promotes from within. If the interviewer tells you that he or she didn't work out, then you know they want somebody highly-qualified who stands a good chance of working out this time around. But if the interviewer avoids or dances around the question, then that could indicate something bad happened. In other words, the answer to this question could tell you if you're going from the frying pan into the fire.

Here are some more questions you may want to ask:

→ Is there an opportunity to grow or move-up? And if so, to what?
→ What benefits do you offer? Medical? Dental? Vision? 401(k)?
→ Who will be the one training me?
→ How long will my training last?

The bottom-line is:

1. *Never* end your interview without asking at least a question or two! Interviews are relatively short and there's always more to know.
2. If you can't think of any questions, then ask the interviewer to confirm or clarify something that was previously said. This way, you're simply double-checking things before you leave.
3. Don't dwell on salary or benefits. You don't want the interviewer to get the sense you're more interested in the money and perks than the job itself. You want the interviewer to see that you enjoy the profession and want a job that's right for you. In other words, job satisfaction is most important; salary and benefits are secondary.

PART 5:

Questions For Students

This section focuses on interview questions that may be asked of students or recent graduates. It may also apply to those of you who are or will be applying for scholarships, grants, or other forms of financial aid.

And even if you're not a student or recent graduate, I would suggest reading this section. That's because you never know what questions an interviewer will ask. Especially if you've gotten some training or went to school, you may be asked about it. So it's a good idea to be prepared!

Now for those of you in school or considering attending school, here's something you should know. The April 25, 2008 release by the U.S. Department of Labor entitled *College Enrollment and Work Activity of 2007 High School Graduates* reported that nearly half of full-time college students were either working, or seeking employment during October 2007. For part-time students, that figure was nearly 84%.

Now these figures may not surprise you, but what may is this. Women were more likely to be the working student. In fact, working women represented 56.6% of students, while their male counterparts stood at 51%. And if you're debating whether furthering your education is worth it, just take a look at this information from the Bureau of Labor Statistics' *Current Population Survey*.

Weekly earnings and Unemployment Rates
FT Employees, ages 25 and older
First Quarter, 2008

Educational level	Unemployment rate	Median weekly earnings	12 month change
Less than high school	7.70%	$435	1.40%
High school graduates, no college	4.80%	$615	2.20%
Some college or associate degree	3.70%	$715	0.70%
Bachelor's degree only	NA	$1,012	5.90%
Bachelor's degree or higher	2.10%	$1,108	7.60%
Advanced degree--Masters & Doctorate	NA	$1,259	4.40%

* From U.S. Department of Labor, Bureau of Labor Statistics' *Current Population Survey*

Why That School?

The question of why you chose to go to a particular school is very similar to "Why do you want to work for our company?" The interviewer is primarily testing your decision-making. After all, you could have gone elsewhere to receive training but made a choice to attend *this* one. The interviewer wants to evaluate your thought process to see exactly how you arrived at your decision. So your reasoning, judgment, and researching abilities are also being evaluated. The important thing to bear in mind is that you must show the interviewer: sound reasoning and judgment, rational or logical thought, and the ability to weight alternatives!

The interviewer must get the feeling you actually put a great deal of thought into it and didn't make a rash or hasty decision. So how do you do this? Well the keys are to show planning, research, and careful weighing of your choices. Then your selection of what appeared to be the best one at the time. Now if you changed schools, you can further highlight your solid decision-making by explaining why you made that change. This shows you re-evaluate things as you go and make appropriate changes when necessary.

In the working world, it's quite common to revisit a decision as new or updated information becomes known. You're demonstrating this ability! Those who won't revisit past decisions if something relevant or important comes to light are being rigid or inflexible. But those who are open to revisiting it are showing flexibility and wise decision-making. How many times have you heard people say they would've made a different choice if they had the newer information at that time? So being open to changing course as new information becomes available is a very important skill in the workplace. This is especially true for those of you currently in or applying for managerial positions!

So you need to clearly explain what it was about *this* particular school that stood-out from all others. Just like you needed to separate yourself from the crowd with the question "Why should I hire you?" You accomplish this by discussing things like the school's:

➔ **Reputation**—Overall and/or relative to your specific training area.

Some are known best for providing training in a specific area. Others are best known for the school's name and not specific departments or subject areas.

➔ **Class size**—With fewer students in class, you sometimes get more individualized or personalized instruction because instructors may have more time to devote to each students.

But that's not always the case. I've taken very large classes with hundreds of students where the professor did get to know each of us and had class time to devote to us. Speaking an educator myself, I can tell you that it all lies in how much information there is to teach and how we structure our classes.

→ **The program itself**—More specialized or concentrated, greater flexibility or choices in picking specific classes or molding your program.

A good example of this is when I was pursuing my undergraduate degree. I had a choice of getting it through either the College of Business or College of Liberal Arts. I chose the liberal arts route because it allowed me to choose from a wider variety of classes in other areas, while still giving me solid training in my major. So my degree included classes that someone going to the College of Business would not have been allowed to take.

→ **Faculty**—Distinguished or known in the field, highly knowledgeable, or extremely helpful, etc.

Some schools have full-time faculty members who are very well known in the community and/or the field. Others have them as part-timers or visiting professors. Many schools have faculty who may not be the biggest names in the world but are extremely knowledgeable in their subject areas and great teachers! Some have more "Ph.D's" on their staff, while others do not.

→ **Instructional methods**—Some schools have a set curriculum or way of instructing students.

For example, I've taught at places where I could structure the class as I saw fit. That meant I could teach and run class in my own way and develop my own lesson materials, homeworks, and tests. I've taught at other places where I didn't have this flexibility. Tests were provided and standardized, lessons were already prepared, and how I taught was decided by the curriculum. Some teachers use only lecture as their way of instructing students. Others combine this with handouts, demonstrations, guest speakers, projects, etc.

→ **Learning modes**—Students today can take classes in a wide variety of formats, including: classroom learning, online classes, CDs and DVDs, audio and video lessons, telecourses, and correspondence classes.

Some prefer one over the other or find it a better means of learning. Others can learn equally well in multiple formats. For instance, I've taught both online and in the classroom. The subject may be the same, but how class operates and the way in which information is presented often differs. In a classroom, I can actually explain things, answer questions, and make adjustments to things right then and there.

But with online learning, students mainly read lessons that have been posted because I'm not right there with them at the time. Does this mean you can't learn or gain as much online as you would in a classroom? No! It's just a different way to learn the same thing.

→ **Resources**—Library, tutoring center or assistance, computer labs, career advising, dining hall, vending machines, etc.

For instance, I've taught at places where there were lots of resources students could turn to and use. I've also taught where the resources were more limited. Some had dining rooms; others had just vending machines. Some had an extensive game room; others did not.

The bottom-line is:

1. Show your thought process by explaining things very clearly. Don't be general! Give very *specific* reasons why you chose this school. Your solid researching of various schools comes in very handy because they help provide those reasons. You need to literally do a side-by-side comparison to show how this school came out on top.

2. Be proud of your choice to highlight your having made a wise decision! That means using a confident voice and having a smile on your face. Never forget that your body language must match your words. If you've changed schools, then explain why you felt it was necessary. That way, the interviewer can see your decision was well thought out.

3. Show this was your choice! In other words, *you* were the one who made the final decision. Even if others had pressured you or something else was involved; it still boils down to the fact that it was ultimately your choice to make.

4. If your choice was based *solely* on the fact that the school was inexpensive and/or the only one that had accepted you, it was your decision to attend. You still could have said no, meaning you weren't going to settle for second-best. But you didn't. That means *you* decided to go there anyway! Right now, you don't look so good because you were short-changing yourself by going to a "lesser" school when it wasn't really where you wanted to be. To turn things around to your advantage, you *must* justify why you chose to remain there or transfer later by using sound reasoning and logical thought!

Why That Major?

The question of selecting a major or area of study tests four things: your personality, decision-making, planning, and researching abilities. In other words, what you decide to get your degree in tells an interviewer a great deal about you as a person.

For example, you can decide to major in something because it's:

→ Where the jobs are right now
→ What everyone else suggests
→ Where you can make the most money
→ What you really enjoy studying or learning about
→ Something you feels is, may, or will be easy

My point is there are many different reasons for selecting a particular major. Your primary motivation is where an interviewer is most interested.

Everybody Suggests This

Let's first look at someone who majors in something mostly because that's what others have suggested. This tells an interviewer you either lacked a sense of direction or couldn't decide for yourself. Either way, it doesn't make you look that good. That's because *you* didn't make the decision! You simply left it up to others to decide for you. An interviewer prefers somebody who can think for himself or herself.

Employers realize that it's common for a 17 to 20 year old to lack direction. But when considering hiring someone for a job, do you really want somebody who doesn't even know what he or she wants? Is it possible this job isn't what he or she really wants? Will this person stay long enough? These are some questions that may run through an interviewer's head, so it's important to show you do have some sense of direction. The more direction you can show, the better you'll look.

You might not have a career in mind yet, but you do need something. Is it work experience? Money? Making your parents happy? Just a way to kill some free time? If you've never worked before, then you should focus on your need to get some experience. The more closely related to your studies, the better. But if not, then you must come across as someone willing to work hard, learn, and remain "long enough." This way, an interviewer will be impressed and see you as a solid investment. This same approach applies to those of you looking for part-time work during breaks or while in school.

Where I can Make Money

Let's focus now on the student who chose a major because that's where the most money can potentially be made. Fact is, college can be expensive! Yes, there are scholarships, grants, and financial aid packages available, but it's still costly to earn a college degree these days. Is it reasonable to assume you'd want a major where you can earn good money? Yes. But when it comes to seeking employment, is this what an interviewer wants to hear? Absolutely not!

Employers understand that money is important to a college student. But would you rather hire someone who likes the profession, or the money? The profession. That's because they'll tend to stay longer and are better workers. Enjoyment of the job and/or profession increases our level of happiness and personal satisfaction. In other words, a happy worker is a more productive one. So it's important for an interviewer to see you aren't just going for the money. He or she must see you chose your field of study because you either like it or thought you would enjoy it.

Where the Jobs are

Now let's turn our attention to the student who chose a major because that's where the jobs were at the time. Employers realize it would be "foolish" to spend lots of money on something that isn't practical. So throwing away money on an education in something where there are few or no jobs would be foolhardy. But the marketplace is ever-changing and what's hot today could become cold tomorrow.

So part of what an interviewer is testing is whether you researched the marketplace. In other words, did you look into the prospects of employment upon graduation? If you're pursuing a Bachelor's Degree, then that's four years of training. A lot can happen in the workplace during that time. The interviewer is interested in whether you were monitoring things while in school to see if your field would still be in demand when graduation approaches. In other words,

- → Did you plan your future ahead of time?
- → Did you research the marketplace to see if jobs would still be there when graduation time comes?
- → Where did you obtain your information?
- → How current is your information?

Personality

As for testing your personality, the interviewer is looking to see if you are cutout for the field. In other words, is your personality a good match with your major? For example, would you say the typical science major is an outgoing, "people-person?" No. Someone majoring in the sciences would tend to be the more quiet and studious type. A person who works more independently doing things like conducting research and performing experiments. Now I'm not saying everyone majoring in sciences like chemistry, biology, etc are like this. But in general, they'll tend to fit this profile.

A student majoring in business would tend to be the exact opposite. Someone who's more outgoing and more of a "people-person." The reason is because the business world is more people-centered. One where communication and human relation skills are very important. This applies to the different areas within business, such as: finance, marketing, management, etc.

Now suppose a student was majoring in electronics or construction. These would require somebody who's more "mechanical." In other words, someone who's good with his or her hands and can build things. This type of person would tend to be very different from someone majoring in say history or literature. How? Construction and electronics students work more with their hands. Those majoring in history or literature work more with their minds. Construction and electronics study is more mechanical, while history and literature is more creative.

My point is that interviewers understand different majors require different personalities. So it's important for the interviewer to feel your personality suits your major. This means you need to make this connection very clear during your interview.

The bottom-line is:

1. It's important to show you gave careful thought to choosing a major. In other words, you didn't make a hasty decision! You thought about it first and chose the one that seemed best for you This shows planning and logical thinking.

2. An interviewer needs to get a sense that you have some direction and have thought about your future. Make the connection between your major and your life clear. This way, the interviewer can see how your schooling fits-in with your career goals and this job. In other words, connect the dots between your personality, your major, your career, the profession, and the job.

3. But what if your major and the job to which you're applying seem to have nothing to do with each other? The key is to realize there's *always* something of relevance. You just have to look very closely to find what that is. There are always elements of work that apply in some respect to your major.

4. For example, you're majoring in English and apply for a part-time job selling tickets at an amusement park. Looks like the two have nothing in common, right? Wrong! There are signs, slogans, and marketing materials that patrons, employees, and vendors will encounter. Your majoring in English has trained you how to write well and ensure things are properly communicated. In other words, there is a connection here! Part of successful interviewing lies making this connection clear to the interviewer.

5. It's important to show an interviewer how your personality matches the major you've chosen. So make this connection clear.

6. If you changed majors, then be prepared to explain your reason(s) why. Make sure you use logical thought and sound reasoning. You should also provide details as to why you felt it was necessary and the right thing to do. This will demonstrate your wise decision-making and ability to readjust.

Your Favorite Class

This question tests your personality and decision-making. An interviewer is very interested in seeing if you:

1. Pick the class where you did best and got your highest grade, or
2. Select the class you actually enjoyed or liked the most

Many applicants will simply jump at the one where they got their highest grade. Now on the surface there doesn't seem to be anything wrong with this. But an interviewer wants to know if it was actually your favorite. That's the real key here! True, we'll tend to work harder and be more motivated in subjects we enjoy. But that doesn't mean we'll necessarily earn good grades in them. The same is true for classes we don't particularly like. We won't automatically do poorly in them just because it's not very enjoyable.

So an interviewer's focus isn't on how well you did, but on what you liked most about it and why. In other words, it's not your performance that's being measured, but rather your ranking of choices and level of enjoyment.

I'll give you a perfect example. I know someone who had taken a computer class and received an *A* in it. Now if you asked her, she would say it was definitely not one of her favorites. She never grasped nor understood any of the material. The only reason for her grade was because she literally memorized the book. So although the material made absolutely no sense, she did well anyway.

My point is that an interviewer wants to know exactly what it was about the class you found most enjoyable. So it doesn't have to be the one where you earned your highest grade. It needs to be the one where you had a really great experience! You must then clearly explain your reason(s) why it was such a wonderful experience.

> **KEY:** Choose the class where you had your best classroom experience and thoroughly enjoyed yourself.

I've had students who didn't really want to be in my class. They were only taking it because it was required for graduation. Yet many of these same students later wound-up enjoying class. That's because it wasn't what they had originally anticipated. They expected it to be useless, boring, theoretical, etc. But to their surprise, it wasn't. So although they didn't want to be there at first, they enjoyed it in the end. Even those who didn't receive the highest grades still liked the class. My point is high marks and class enjoyment don't always go together!

An interviewer doesn't really care how well you did in that class. The main focus is on why you enjoyed it. So it's perfectly fine to mention the class where your performance wasn't so great, but you really enjoyed yourself. For example, if you got a *D* in the it but had a highly dynamic instructor who made class very interesting, then it's perfectly understandable why you would have enjoyed it. The instructor made things interesting and the material "came alive!"

So why did you get a lower grade? Well there are many legitimate reasons that have nothing to do with goofing-off or not trying hard. For instance:

→ It could have been an extremely tough class
→ Maybe you were working long hours and didn't have as much time to devote to class as you would have liked
→ The instructor may have been an extremely tough grader—no curving of grades, no partial credit, etc.
→ The textbook was a "monster" to read, meaning it was tedious and not very helpful without somebody there to explain things
→ There may have been a family crisis or emergency that preoccupied you and took valuable time away from your studies
→ Your instructor wasn't available to answer questions or provide assistance

My point is that it doesn't matter if you did well. What's important is that you had a very positive experience in class. Your classroom performance is a totally separate issue!

The bottom-line is:

1. Don't automatically select the class where you did your best because the focus here is on *why* you enjoyed it. In other words, performance and class enjoyment are two separate issues. While they may go together, the interviewer here is only interested in your level of enjoyment.
2. Use sound reasoning to explain exactly why you like the class more than others. Was your teacher really great? Was it because class was better than expected? Was it the way in which the class was run? Were your classmates much nicer and/or more helpful? In other words, provide *details* so the interviewer can understand why this class was so enjoyable.
3. Be sure you show enthusiasm when speaking. If you don't look and sound impressed and happy, then the interviewer will question it. In other words, look and sound the part or you won't come across as believable. It's very important the interviewer sees your *true* reason(s) for picking that particular class. Otherwise, you're being dishonest and that hurts you.

Lowest Grade

Now here's a question I'm sure plenty of you don't want to be asked. After all, who wants to admit they didn't so well? But from an interviewer's standpoint, it's a very good question to ask. It measures a candidate's problem-solving ability, which is exactly what's being tested.

Employers understand that students don't do well in everything. There's always something we find a little harder or struggle with. An interviewer is very interested in knowing what those areas are. But more importantly, your reaction!

For example:

- → Did you try your best to do well?
- → Did you devote enough time to it?
- → Did you follow your teacher's instructions?
- → Did you complete everything on-time?
- → Did you seek-out assistance or ask for help?
- → Did you pay attention in class?
- → Did you read things carefully?

To an interviewer, poor performance is just another problem that needs to be resolved. So the focus is on your ability to diagnose and deal with the problem. In other words:

- → Did you recognize you had a problem with not doing well?
- → What step(s) did you take to improve your grade?
- → Did your grade improve as a result of your action(s)?

It's extremely important you tell the interviewer why you struggled and exactly how you handled it. In other words, show the interviewer that you:

- → Identified the problem of not doing so well
- → Looked for a good way to improve your performance and grade
- → Took action to do better
- → Noticed improvement as a direct result your having taken action

KEY #1:   Identify your problem, take action, and show improvement

Let's assume you didn't do so well in class because you either:

➜ Didn't try very hard
➜ Hated the class and/or you teacher
➜ Didn't really care about the class because it was outside your major
➜ Missed several class meetings, assignments, tests, etc.
➜ Found the class and/or teacher extremely boring

Would you really want to admit any of these to an interviewer? Do they make you look impressive and scream "Hire me?" No, which is exactly why most applicants will come-up with something else. But do reasons like these actually hurt you? Well that all depends on whether you repeated your mistake or learned from it. Just remember that on the job, you may:

➜ Work with people you don't particularly like but have to deal with anyway
➜ Have aspects of your job that aren't the most interesting nor enjoyable
➜ Be asked to do something you don't like or wasn't in your job description
➜ Encounter or work with somebody who's boring, seemingly unfriendly, or not very talkative

My point is that all of your learning environment situations relate directly to the working world. The interviewer is trying to determine whether your behavior in school will be the same on the job. In other words, "You didn't do that well in school, so maybe you won't do well on the job." This is why you must show you're capable of successfully identifying and resolving problems!

KEY #2:   Show you've learned from your mistakes

Human beings aren't perfect and do make mistakes. So it's extremely important for an interviewer to see that you've *learned* from your mistake(s). Not learning from past mistakes will really hurt your chances of getting hired. Why? Because it means we'll do it again and employers don't want or keep people who repeatedly make the same mistake(s). In other words, they'll only allow a certain number of mistakes. It all depends upon the severity of the error—minor errors being tolerated more than major ones.

Interviewers also realize that someone age 16 to 20 is still "young" and probably doesn't know everything about the working world. So they're given more latitude. This means that "blowing-off" school or class once in a while goes with being young and immature. But an interviewer *must* now see that you've "grown-up!" You have to show that you've:

➜ Taken responsibility and are more mature in your attitude and thinking.
➜ Faced the consequences of your past mistake(s).
➜ Learned not to do it again in the future.

In other words, you're a different person from the one who made those mistakes. Today, you are more mature, professional, and responsible. An interviewer must see these positive qualities from you in order to turn things around in your favor. That's because those mistakes you made before won't be tolerated nor admired in the workplace!

The bottom-line is:

1. Show the interviewer you understand the problem-solving process: identify the real problem, find possible solutions, select the best course of action, implement it, and check the results to see if it worked. If so, wonderful! But if not, then re-evaluate and adjust accordingly. Failure to do this means you're willing to live with a problem and in the workplace, that's unacceptable. Problems must be handled!
2. Take responsibility for your poor performance. The proper attitude is to admit you made a mistake. In other words, be honest and say "I messed-up." Putting the blame on something else is shirking your responsibility, and that doesn't impress anyone.
3. Explain how you've learned from your past mistakes so they won't be repeated. This demonstrates your ability to grow and improve. Companies want employees who can learn, grow, and improve!
4. To be responsible on the job, you have to take responsibility for your own life. That's because if you're not responsible in your own life, then maybe you won't be responsible on the job. Remember, our behaviors in other areas may repeat themselves on the job. Employers want people who are responsible!

Your Grades or GPA

This can be a pretty tough question for students who's grades aren't so great. Those with higher grade point averages (GPAs) are proud to say they're doing well in school. They feel it's something that will really impress an interviewer and make themselves look good. Students with lower grades worry an interviewer won't be impressed by their less than stellar performance in school. So they'll often dance around the issue in their responses. In other words, they'll de-emphasize their lower GPA by focusing on something else.

KEY #1:   Grades don't measure intelligence and capabilities

Many job seekers incorrectly assume that grades measure how smart or intelligent someone is. This just isn't the case! Yes, high marks can be an indicator that a candidate is probably smart. But does a student with lower grades mean he or she isn't smart or capable of doing the job? No! There are many reasons why a student might struggle in school that have nothing to do with one's intellect. For instance:

→ Teachers who don't explain things very well. In other words, those who take the attitude of "Just read your book!"
→ A textbook that's extremely tough to read and comprehend—a "monster"
→ Having a job that involves working long hours and cuts into your study time
→ Dealing with a personal or family situation that demands a lot of your time and may preoccupy you
→ Early on, you spent more time partying instead of studying because you didn't know how to effectively manage your time back then. As a result, your grades suffered

My point is there are other reasons for poor performance besides lacking intelligence or the ability to do well. So grades aren't a very good measure of one's capabilities and intelligence.

KEY #2:   Your effort counts most!

There are many people throughout history who weren't the best students in the world. Yet they turned-out just fine and became productive members of society. Albert Einstein flunked math and became one of the world's most brilliant scientists. Bill Gates dropped out of school and became head of Microsoft. So low grades or dropping-out won't automatically hurt your chances of becoming successful. An interviewer is far more interested in hearing you tried your best.

But what if you fell into the trap of partying too much and your grades suffered as a result? It all comes down to your not managing your time very well. How can you turn this around and make yourself look better? You need to do two things:

1. Take full responsibility for your actions
2. Show the interviewer that you've learned from your mistakes.

Interviewers realize how common it is for students to party because it's probably the first time they've been out on their own. But there comes a time when you must realize that life isn't one big party. A large part of growing-up includes making mistakes along the way. Your education needs to be taken seriously or you may not graduate and/or find a decent job. An interviewer needs to see you've grasped this concept! He or she must also see you've become more adult in your thinking and behavior.

Tip: A great way to demonstrate this is by showing how your grades have improved because you concentrated more on your studies.

In other words, you took action to improve your performance in school and it worked! This makes you look better because you've identified and solved a problem. The interviewer will now see you as somebody who:

→ Noticed a problem
→ Took corrective action
→ Worked hard
→ Is a good problem-solver

KEY #3:   Grades and school choice go together

Now it's your turn to play interviewer. Take a good look at the below table. It provides information about two students who've applied for the exact same job. They both have the same major and have completed three years of schooling. Who would you say is the better candidate?

	Student 1	Student 2
GPA	4.0 (A+)	3.5 (B+)
School	University of Wisconsin	Princeton University
Major	Business	Business
Years Completed	3	3

Some might be thinking it's the one with the 4.0 because this person's grades are obviously better. Others may be leaning towards the one with the 3.5 because that person is attending Princeton. So it becomes a trade-off between the candidate's grades and the school's reputation. When deciding whom to hire, interviewers may consider how grades from different schools compare. This is something that job seekers should realize and understand. So who is the better candidate in my example? Well that all depends on the interviewer. One may feel that Princeton is a better school and a 3.5 from there is equal to, or better than a 4.0 from the University of Wisconsin. Another may feel they're both good schools. In other words, it's a personal judgment call!

Now this doesn't automatically mean you should attend the best schools. A school's reputation isn't the only factor in selecting and rating a school. Things like cost, atmosphere, class size, resources, etc are also important. Yet today, some parents today are literally bankrupting themselves in order to send their children to the top Ivy League schools. They're hoping it'll improve their child's job hunting success upon graduation. The attitude is basically this: an Ivy League education carries more clout, which means you'll either get a job faster or a better one.

One problem with this strategy is that interviewers may also rank and compare grades and reputations of Ivy League schools. In other words, one may feel that Columbia isn't quite as good as Stamford. Someone else may feel they're equal. Another might say that Stamford is better. So you may find yourself right back where you started! Another problem is the interviewer could feel your Ivy League education means you'll want even more money or prestige. An interviewer may also begin to wonder how long you'll remain on the job or with the company. Or if you're motivated more by the money and prestige than a love of the job or profession.

My suggestion is to choose a school that's right for you! One that is both reputable and offers solid training in your area of interest. Reputations may vary, but getting an education is *always* a good thing. It shows that you're trainable and willing to learn. Employers want people who exhibit these qualities. The point is to demonstrate you made a conscious decision and feel you got a solid education. What matters most to an interviewer is knowing that:

➜ Your school is legit and provides quality education
➜ You worked hard in school and did your best

In other words, the quality of your education and your best efforts count the most! The bottom-line is:

1. Grades aren't a true measure of one's intelligence and abilities. A student might struggle in school for a variety of legitimate reasons other than he or she isn't smart.
2. It's hard to compare grades from different schools because personal attitudes and feelings may get in the way. This means a lower score from a tougher school may offset a higher grade from an easier school. So bear in mind that an interviewer may rank and compare grades and a school's reputation as a way to level the playing field.
3. What matters most is the quality of education, not grades or the school's reputation!
4. Anyone with a solid education and the needed skills has the potential to do well. Your school provided the quality training and you feel you have the necessary skills. Therefore, you feel you'd do a good job if hired.

Who Paid for School?

You may be thinking an interviewer doesn't really need to know this. Correct, he or she doesn't. So why are you being asked this question? It's a test to see if you know what's truly important.

> **KEY #1**: Gaining knowledge matters most

Exactly how you paid for your schooling isn't relevant. What's important was your decision to get an education! This is exactly what the interviewer needs to hear. You either:

→ Made a personal choice to expand your mind and get some training
→ Were willing to return to school to gain additional knowledge that will help you become a better employee

In the workplace, additional training often leads to greater success. That's why many companies have employees go through professional development training. It's a way to keep them current and improve their level of knowledge so they can do better on the job. Whether you chose to go to school on your own or were sent there by your employer doesn't really matter. What matters is you're willingness to be trained!

> **KEY #2**: School requires commitment and hard work

Going to school, especially while working, takes a commitment in both time and money. An interviewer needs to see that you fully-intend to complete your training. For example, going to school for a Bachelor's Degree as a full-time student who isn't working may take four years. But working full-time and going to school part-time may take six or seven. Either way, the interviewer must see your commitment to finishing. This shows good decision-making and a high degree of both motivation and dedication!

If an employer sends you for training and pays for it, they expect you to complete it! When I worked as a Software Trainer, I had students in class who were there because the boss sent them. Sometimes, the boss would check to make sure they actually showed-up rather than blowing it off and missing work. Did these students know about that? Most often, no! So you must show that if an employer sends you for training, you're willing to go and will complete it. Because the workplace is dynamic and changes, employees will need some sort of training from time-to-time. An employee who's unwilling to do it won't last very long! In others, learning really never ends!

Tip: If you're working and going to school, then highlight your time-management skills by showing how you *effectively* juggle school and work. In other words, explain how you're able to manage both well. This demonstrates your ability to multitask.

The bottom-line is:

1. Understand it's not important who paid for school. What's important is getting an education!
2. If you're currently in school, then explain you fully-intend to complete your training and believe going to school was the right thing to do.
3. If you've already graduated, then explain how your schooling has given you the education and skills needed to succeed in this job and/or profession.
4. Realize an employer may send you may back for additional training. Show your understanding that professional development and keeping "current" in the workplace are important. The interviewer is testing your understanding of the concept that work is dynamic and learning never ends!

PART 6:

Illegal Questions

This section focuses on questions that are considered to be illegal or off-limit. In other words, in 99.99% of cases, an interviewer should not ask you them. The main reason why certain questions are considered illegal is to prevent discriminatory hiring. So it's to protect you, the job seeker!

But even with this protection in place, I feel it's important you prepare for the possibility of being asked an illegal question. That's because you may run into an interviewer out there who ask them for any number of reasons.

What's Legal and Illegal

There are several categories of illegal questions. These include:

→ Race
→ Religion
→ Sex
→ Family
→ National origin
→ Marital status
→ Garnishments
→ Arrest record
→ Disability
→ Military service
→ Credit history

For example, an interviewer should not ask you questions like:

1. What country are you from?
2. You sound like you're from Japan. Am I correct?
3. Are you single?
4. How many children do you have?
5. Do you plan on having kids?
6. Are you pregnant?
7. Have you ever been arrested?
8. Ever been suspected of a crime?
9. I see you're in a wheelchair, what's wrong with you?
10. Do you have any disabilities?
11. Are you Christian or Protestant?
12. Were you honorably discharged from the military?
13. Where did you learn to speak Spanish?

Why are all of these considered illegal? Because they open the door to discrimination when the only thing that really matters is your ability to perform the functions of the job. For instance:

➔ Does your being from another country mean you're not qualified to handle the job? No. So asking about your country of origin isn't relevant to your ability to do the job. It opens the door to discrimination against non-native born applicants. It can also discriminate against native-born candidates who are of a particular ethnicity or race.

➔ Asking about your accent could reveal what country you're from or what ethnicity you are. This could lead to discrimination against candidates from that country or of that ethnicity.

➔ Questions about where you learned to speak or write a particular language might discriminate against native-born speakers from a particular country. It could also discriminate against a particular race or ethnic group.

➔ Could you perform the job regardless of your marital status? Yes. And so your marital status has no bearing on your ability to handle the job. Therefore, it may discriminate against candidates of other marital status.

➔ Does having children automatically mean you can't meet the job's requirements? No. You can still be qualified and fulfill the job requirements. So family status isn't relevant to your performance of the job! Asking about family can discriminate against a married or single parent applicant.

➔ Does being pregnant automatically prevent you from performing your job? No. It's possible you could still perform the job even if you are pregnant. Asking about pregnancy or future child plans discriminates against female candidates.

➔ Just because you've been arrested or suspected of a crime, does it mean you definitely committed it? No. You may be totally innocent! Besides, it has no bearing on your ability to perform the job itself. And because statistics have shown a disproportionate number of minorities getting arrested, it could lead to discrimination against a minority applicant.

➔ Does being in a wheelchair or having a disability automatically mean you can't handle the job? No. It's possible you can still meet the job requirements. So asking about one's disability discriminates against the disabled. It presumes this person would have difficulty or be unable to perform the job when he or she may actually be able to do it.

So to prevent qualified individuals from being discriminated against, certain areas are considered off-limits by interviewers. Yet this doesn't mean you won't run into an interviewer who asks an illegal question. True, the vast majority of interviewers know what's all right to ask and what is not. But there could be reasons for the illegal question. The interviewer may:

➔ Not realize it's illegal
➔ Just want to see your reaction to it
➔ Perceive in his or her own mind a legitimate reason for asking
➔ Presume the applicant won't know it's illegal and will simply answer it

For example, suppose you're applying for a sales position that involves extensive traveling. An interviewer may personally feel that a candidate without a spouse or children may be more available to travel. So it's not having anything against married people or those with families. It's a matter of perceived availability to travel a lot. In other words, this interviewer assumes a single person without somebody to take care of will be able to travel more and/or at the last minute.

But let me make it perfectly clear, this is totally illegal! You see, just because somebody is married or has children doesn't mean he or she can't travel extensively. Arrangements could be made to workaround a spouse or family. So this candidate may be just as available as the single person!

Now there are various legal questions that an interviewer can ask you. Examples include:

1. Are you authorized to work in this country (the U.S.)?
2. Can you meet or fulfill the job requirements?
3. Are or were you in the military?
4. Can you submit verification of your legal right to work in this country?
5. This job requires extensive travel. Can you do this?
6. The hours of this job are Thursday to Sunday, 10 AM to 3 PM. Can you work this shift?

These aren't considered illegal because they're more general in nature. In other words, you're not being asked what country you're from. You're only being asked if are legally allowed to work in this country. The interviewer isn't asking if you have some sort of disability, are married, or have children. He or she is merely asking if you can meet the job requirements.

You're not being asked about your performance in the military. The interviewer's only asking if you ever served in the military. And you're not being asked if your religion prevents you from working on certain days. The interviewer is asking if you are available to work a particular shift. So questions like these that don't have an inherent bias or are blatantly discriminatory are considered legal and all right to ask.

To help further reduce and combat bias and discrimination, every job has what's called a *BFOQ*. That stands for *Bona Fide Occupational Qualifications*. For every job, the BFOQ spells-out exactly what's required in order to perform the job. So the BFOQ for an inventory position may specify a minimum weight lifting requirement.

For example, if you're going to be handling heavier items, the BFOQ may say the applicant needs to be able to lift 50 lbs. This means that any candidate applying for this job must have the ability to lift 50 lbs. So whether you're a male or female applicant, you're considered qualified as long as you can lift 50 lbs.

Now you may be saying this is unfair because a male applicant could be stronger than a female applicant. And that may be the case. But due to safety concerns, having a weight requirement here is valid. The last thing an employer wants is someone regularly lifting heavy items hurting themselves. So the weigh requirement is a way to make sure a candidate could perform the job without injury. And since lifting and moving heavy items is such an integral part of the job, having a weight requirement is considered legal and non-discriminatory.

The same applies to someone who wants to be a firefighter. Because the job involves rescuing people from burning building, accidents, and other disasters, that person has to be able to lift and carry heavy weights. So a BFOQ may state the candidate must be able to carry 100 lbs at least 20 feet. After all, the last thing anybody wants is a firefighter coming to your rescue and not being able to get you out! Again, it's an integral part of the job and a public health and safety issue.

It's also all right to have an age requirement for jobs like Bartender. To serve alcohol, the applicant must be of legal age. So the BFOQ may say that a candidate applying for this job must be at least 21 years old. This would prevent an underage individual from working as a Bartender.

Employment Laws

There are several laws in place to protect job seekers from discriminatory hiring practices. Some of the ones you should be aware of are:

→ Title VII of the Civil Rights Act of 1964
→ The Civil Rights Act of 1991
→ Executive Order 11246
→ The Americans with Disabilities Act (ADA)
→ The Age Discrimination in Employment Act of 1967 (ADEA)
→ The Pregnancy Discrimination Act of 1978
→ The Fair Labor Standards Act (FLSA)

Title VII of the Civil Rights Act of 1964 makes it's illegal for an employer to discriminate against candidates on the basis of race, gender, religion, or national origin. And it applies to employers with at least 15 employees.

The Civil Rights Act of 1991 expanded protection by making it illegal for employers to treat test scores of minority applicants differently as a way to increase the pool of minority applicants. In other words, an employer can't use a lower standard for minority candidates and a higher one for non-minorities.

Executive Order 11246 applies to employers having at least $10,000 in federal contracts. It extended Title VII protection to these employers, regardless of how many employees they have. And it requires these employers to have a written affirmative action plan.

The Americans with Disability Act makes it illegal for an employer to discriminate against someone who's physically or mentally disabled, yet qualified. It allows the applicant to request a reasonable accommodation be made to work around his or her disability. It also places substantial limits on what employers can ask if there is a perceived disability. And it prohibits an employer from conducting a physical exam prior to your being offered the job.

Notice how I said *reasonable* accommodation! The law doesn't say an employer must accommodate your disability. It merely says that it has to be something reasonable. So asking an employer to spend $100,000 on special equipment or to construct new workspace may not be viewed as reasonable. However, spending $1000 may be seen as perfectly reasonable. The definition of what's reasonable is still something that courts have been wrestling with. But it has to be something that won't place an undue hardship on the employer.

And the accommodation request must come from the applicant! In other words, you must ask for an accommodation to be made and specify what that would be. For example, if you're blind, you may request an ADA reader be installed to read the words on your screen. If you're wheelchair bound, then you might ask for extra time to get around and make it back from lunch. Or you may ask for an ergonomic keyboard if you have

Carpal Tunnel Syndrome or Repetitive Stress Injury (RSI). But remember, the request must come from you, not the employer!

The Age Discrimination in Employment Act was put into law to prevent discrimination against older, yet qualified individuals. It makes it illegal for an employer to discriminate against a qualified candidate just because he or she is age 40 or older. It also places limitations on mandatory retirement. And it applies to labor unions, employment agencies, and employers with at least 20 employees.

The Pregnancy Discrimination Act expanded Title VII protection to prevent discrimination towards pregnant women and women having childbirth, or related medical issues. It also requires these women be treated the same as other employees when it comes to benefits and employment conditions.

The Fair Labor Standards Act sets the federal minimum wage level and how overtime pay works. It also discusses the use of child labor and includes rules for classifying employees as being exempt or non-exempt. *Exempt* employees are those who are straight salaried. That means they aren't paid based upon the number of hours they work. By contrast, *non-exempt* employees are hourly employees paid based upon the number of hours they work. If they work over 40 hours a week, then they are entitled to overtime at a rate of time-and-a-half. This is how it works in Washington State. But in some states, you are paid time-and-a-half if you work more than 8 hours per day.

One last law you may want to know about is called the *Genetic Information Nondiscrimination Act of 2008* (*GINA*). Years in the making, and signed into law by President George W. Bush on May 21, 2008, this new law will make it illegal for employers to discriminate based upon genetic testing. In other words, if you or a family member get a DNA or other genetic test, it prevents employers and health insurers from discriminating against you should those results become known to them. So this law is intended to protect you from the potential negative impact of your genetic information becoming public. And it's designed to protect your own genetic information and that of your family (family history).

Why? Because it's possible an employer or health insurer might discriminate against you on the basis that a family member's genetic information is deemed negative. For instance, it would protect you against discrimination from having a family history of adult onset diabetes. It also prevents an employer from buying, requiring, or requesting genetic information, except for certain reasons. And effective May 28, 2008, it increases the amount a company can be fined for violating child laws by $1,000 per violation.

I should point out that GINA won't take effect right away, but rather one year from now. In May 2009, the part that protects you from health insurance discrimination goes into effect. The protection against employer discrimination won't take effect until November 2009. And it doesn't cover those of you in the military. However, there are a bunch of state laws that provide protection, along with partial protection contained within other US employment laws. But what GINA does accomplish is provide a minimim standard for the wide variety of state laws that are out there. And provides protection to those in states where there were no pre-existing state laws.

For instance, Florida only protects those of you who have a particular trait (gene). GINA expands this protection to all others. Some states protected just your own genetic information. GINA extends it to your family history. But what I found interesting was that Arizone doesn't even prevent employers from requiring or requesting employees to undergo genetic testing. GINA would prohibit this unless certain exceptions are met. And states like Massachusetts, New York, and Oregon already prevent employers from requiring or requesting genetic test results, and from discriminating on the basis of it.

Handling Illegal Questions

How should you handle illegal questions. Well some experts suggest you outright refuse to answer. Others suggest letting the interviewer know it's an illegal question. However, I suggest you *never* refuse to answer. That's because an interviewer may think you have something to hide or are an overly-sensitive person.

I also suggest not throwing it back at the interviewer by saying it's illegal. The interviewer may not take kindly to it and may even feel you're questioning his or her intelligence. Are you saying the interviewer's not smart enough to know what's legal and what's not? Do you know the law better than he or she does? Are you questioning the interviewer's qualifications? In other words, I think you may be opening "Pandora's Box" and possibly antagonizing the interviewer. Either of these won't make you look impressive and could hurt your chances.

Instead, I suggest you mention that the question he or she asked isn't important. What is truly important is that you are fully-capable and ready to handle the job. With my approach, you're being "nicer" and showing you understand what really matters—Being qualified to handle the job!

The bottom-line is:

1. Be nice in your response by not refusing to answer nor throwing it back in the interviewer's face.
2. Politely say you don't feel the answer to that question is overly important.
3. Mention your opinion that what really matters is your ability to perform the job.
4. Follow-up with your experience, education, and any other capabilities you possess that will make you successful in the position. This way, your linking your capabilities to job performance.
5. If you wish to file a formal complaint, you can do so by visiting the Equal Employment Opportunity Commission's (EEOC) website at *www.eeoc.gov*.

Appendix A: Sample Cover Letter

Jason Smith
123 Main Street
Seattle, WA 98101
(206) 555-1111

January 5, 2008

Mike Johnson, Personnel Director
Suregood Security Company
300 Allenwood Place
Seattle, WA 98109

Dear Mr. Johnson:

I am writing to see if your company can use somebody with 5 years experience in the security business and have enclosed my resume for your review.

As an extremely responsible and dedicated employee, I have worked hard to protect company personnel and property from theft, damage, and harm. To accomplish this goal, I would regularly check identifications and keep a watchful eye on the people around me.

In addition, I would always treat people with respect. And because of my vigilance, nothing has ever been stolen. Nor has anyone been harmed or felt threatened during my shifts! I have also successfully completed an in-house security training program. And have been trained in CPR.

I am very confident Mr. Johnson that I could bring this same level of protection to you. You can reach me at (206) 555-1111 to discuss my desire in greater detail. Or to schedule an interview.

Thank you very much for your time and consideration. I look forward to hearing from you soon.

Sincerely,

Jason Smith

Enc.

Appendix B:
Sample Chronological Resume

Mary Ellison

295 Ridgemont Avenue
Bergenfield, NJ 07621

Home: (201) 555-8310   **Cell**: (201) 555-1403   **E-mail**: mellison8@cox.net

A highly experienced professional with 3 years of supervisory expertise and 4 years providing support

Professional Work Experience

Addison Industries   **Office Manager**   **2005-Present**
- Supervise 4 office assistants
- Provide assistance and quality support to 2 Vice Presidents
- Help create the budgets and forecasts
- Process vendor contracts and renewals
- Maintain calendars and schedule appointments, including follow-ups
- Coordinate vacation schedules
- Handle billing
- Screen and hire new support staff
- Process timesheets and handout payroll checks
- Take and distribute meeting minutes
- Type letters and reports
- Sort and distribute the mail

McKinley and Chase   **Administrative Assistant**   **2001-2005**
- Typed letters and various reports
- Handled customer questions and complaints
- Scheduled appointments
- Worked on special projects

Education

Montclair State College   A.A.S. in Business   2001

Appendix C:
Sample Functional Resume

Mike Racine

433 Lindbloom Court
Dallas, TX 33165
(413) 555-1666
mrae31@gmail.com

Skills and Abilities

- Extremely responsible
- Very trustworthy
- Highly motivated
- A good communicator
- Made the Dean's List
- Took classes in management, accounting, and business math
- Knowledge of basic managerial principles
- Able to work independently when necessary
- A strong team-player
- Wrote a detailed analysis of a case study I was assigned to read
- Wrote letters and setup mail-merges using Microsoft Word
- Used MS Excel to setup and format spreadsheets and databases
- Can search the Internet to research and gather information
- Basic knowledge of MS Access

Education

Texas A&M University	B.S., Business Management	2006-2010

Appendix D:
Sample Combination Resume

Mary Ellison
295 Ridgemont Avenue
Bergenfield, NJ 07621

Home: (201) 555-8310   **Cell:** (201) 555-1403   **E-mail:** mellison8@cox.net

A highly experienced professional with 3 years of supervisory expertise and 4 years providing support

Skills and Abilities

- Type 55 wpm
- Extremely responsible, trustworthy, and motivated
- Provide the highest level of customer support
- Successfully resolve problems and meet deadlines
- Have strong communication and leadership skills
- Am very well-organized and personable
- Manage tasks and my time very well
- Proven ability to work alone and part of a team

Professional Work Experience

Addison Industries   **Office Manager**   **2005-Present**

- Supervise 4 office assistants
- Provide assistance and quality support to 2 Vice Presidents
- Help prepare budgets and forecasts
- Maintain calendars and schedule follow-up appointments
- Take meeting minutes
- Sort and distribute the mail

McKinley and Chase   **Administrative Assistant**   **2001-2005**

- Prepared correspondence and various reports
- Handled customer questions and scheduled appointments

Education

Montclair State College   A.A.S. in Business   2001

Appendix E:
Ways to Condense Your Resume

Here are some helpful tips for those of you who want to condense (shorten) your resume. For example, you want to try to fit everything onto one page. Or just make it shorter. Maybe you want to try something different to see how it looks. Either way, these tips will help you out.

→ Play with your margins

One thing I've noticed is that many people will use wider margins than they actually have to. So one thing that's very easy to do is use smaller margins. The smallest you should go is a half inch on all sides—top, bottom, left, and right. That's within the printable area of all printers. However, some can print with margins as low as 0.3 to 0.35. The point is to make your resume look centered on the page. That gives it a nice visual effect and is more pleasing on the eye.

→ Adjust your heading style

Depending on your resume's formatting, this tip may or may not apply to you. In many job hunting resources, you'll see resumes with headings on the left and all the information on the right. Using this format wastes a lot of space!

I suggest reformatting your resume so your headings are centered and your information is listed underneath. This will shorten your resume's length by recouping that wasted space. It will also allow you to possibly add or expand what's already on there. And that can make your resume even more effective!

→ Group and consolidate

On chronological resumes, it's pretty common to list the same thing multiple times. For example, you did filing in each of your jobs. Many will put *filing* underneath each job, which is repetitive. To shorten your resume's length, cut it out of one or two jobs. In other words, having it listed once or twice is sufficient. Besides, employers know that filing is part of many support jobs. That makes it a given to positions like assistant, admin assistant, clerk, etc. So you don't have to repeat yourself!

→ Revise your objective

Depending on your objective or career summary, you might be able reword it so it's not so lengthy. Or remove it entirely to free up even more space. You see, an objective *isn't* required. So you have flexibility in deciding whether to include it or not. And if yours is so broad that it really doesn't add much, then delete it.

For instance: *Looking for a position that uses my skills and abilities and provides a challenge.* Of course we want to use our skills! Challenges come with every job because a problem can arise at anytime or people can come and go. So they're givens! This makes your objective in my professional opinion useless and a waste of valuable space. So kill it in this case.

If your objective is more along the lines of *Seeking a position in customer service*, then try rewording. Try something like *A customer service position*. In other words, shorten the number of words or the length of words.

➔ Play with your font sizes

The smallest font size that's readable enough is 10 pt. Now I'm not telling you to use this size on everything! Just use it for your information within certain sections. *Headings* must be the same! But how the information is structured under each can be different.

For example, you can make your information in all sections—objective, work history, education, etc—10 point. Or you could adjust the education section only. Both are perfectly acceptable because the sections are independent of each other.

If that's close to a page, but a little bit over, then you can make your headings 10 point bolded to standout. The main thing is to make your headings different from your information so they are more noticeable and standout.

➔ Adjust font names

There are tons of fonts available on computers today. But not all of them are good for resumes! However, you do have several choices available with each one looking a bit different. Some fonts are larger; others make their letters and numbers look closer together. My point is you can substitute one for the other. That's provided everything is still readable enough!

Times Roman or *Times New Roman* is a smaller font. Here, the letters look smaller and closer together. *Courier* is a larger font where the letters more spaced out. In other words, the letters look wider and bigger. *Arial* is even bigger, yet the letters are closer together.

But they are all readable enough and are suitable for resumes. So you may be able to swap one for the other to free up some space and cut down the length. And once again, you don't have to do this for everything unless you want to! You can do it only for your heading. Or just to your information. Or even to a particular section's information.

➔ Redo your contact information layout

There are many acceptable ways to list your name and contact information on a resume. Some have their name on one line, street address on the next, city on the third, and phone or e-mail on the last. In other words, you could be using 4 to 5 lines just for all this!

To lower the amount of space it uses, you may want to revamp how it looks. If you have your phone and e-mail on separate lines, combine them. In other words, have one on the left and the other on the right of the same line. That removes one whole line.

You could also try putting your street address, city, state, and zip on a single line. Then do the same for your phone or email. This reduces your contact information down to just 3 lines, including your name.

Or make your street address, city, state, and zip fill two lines on the left. Then, put your phone and e-mail on the same two lines, but on the right. With your name, this takes up just 3 lines of space. I've even seen some resumes where your entire contact info, including your name is on a single line! But that to me is a last resort.

Appendix F: Letter of Resignation

You may find it strange to have a letter of resignation in a book about job hunting. But if you're working now and find something else, you'll need to leave your current job. Yet many people don't write a letter of resignation, say the wrong or inappropriate things, or leave important parts out. So I've decided to help you and truly make this book an A to Z on job hunting.

Now some experts say a resignation letter isn't always necessary. For example, you feel you're being forced out. Or are leaving under very bad circumstances. Or being totally disrespected. But I disagree with them and here's why.

Yes, you may not like the job, company, or customers. Or even your boss or coworkers. But it's mean of you not to leave as a true professional. And that's something that can haunt you later. How? When it comes reference time and your company doesn't give you a good one. Or worse, none at all. And the worst of them all, not coding you for rehire! That means the company would *never*, in a million years, rehire you for *anything*.

However, resigning professionally and not badmouthing them in your resignation letter may accomplish two important things. First, you may get a decent reference out of them for resigning more professionally. And second, they may code you for rehire for the very same reason. This is what I feel those experts are not taking into account. And why I feel it's best to write a nice and proper letter of resignation. To me, anything that improves your chances of success should be done!

Now here's a common mistake. People will say they're leaving, but fail to mention when their last day will be. You may be thinking, "I'll just say it to my boss or somebody else." What if somebody forgets? Or pretends you didn't say anything? It's your word against theirs. And who do you think the company will believe more? Them! But writing a resignation letter with a specific date or timeframe protects yourself because it's right there in print. And time starts with your letter's date.

How much time should you give? Well it's customary to give two weeks notice. This is to provide enough time for your boss to work around your leaving and begin making arrangements to find a replacement. So if you can, do this. But there may be times when this isn't possible. For example, your new employer needs you to start earlier. Or you want to "get the heck out!". Giving less time isn't your best option because it may leave your boss in a lurch. And makes you seem like the bad one. But you do have to work around the new employer. So if you just can't give two weeks, then you can't.

As I mentioned earlier, it's never a good idea to badmouth anyone! This is another common mistake. People will state their real reasons for leaving. And they'll be very mean and nasty. After all, if they treated you badly, why be nice? Well that's a mistake in my professional opinion! Remember, you want to leave on good terms and perhaps get a reference out of them later on. So I suggest being nicer in your letter by toning it down. For example, don't say something like "I'm so glad to get outta here!" or "You treated me so badly that I hope everybody else leaves too!"

If they provided some training or helped you out up to a point, then you can thank them for it. If you like some of the people you work with, then you can say how much you'll miss working with them. You can also do this if you liked the customers or clients. You could even mention that you'll miss working being a part of the company.

This is useful when you like the company overall but not your particular office or boss. In other words, focus on the more positive aspects of your job. And if you can't give two weeks notice, then be sure to mention it's because your new employer needs you to start sooner. This way, your boss knows it wasn't your decision to leave earlier. You had no choice but to work around the needs of your new employer.

One last mistake is forgetting to sign your letter. This is a business document that goes into your personnel file. Without a signature, it's meaningless because somebody else could have written it. But your signature on it verifies it's authenticity. And make sure you give human resource (personnel) a copy of your letter so it can be placed into your permanent file.

Here is a sample letter of resignation.

Kevin Michaels
1255 Eastern Way
Bellevue, WA 98003

January 14, 2008

Jack Ryan, Manager
Stone Roofing and Supply
1832 NE 140th Street
Seattle, WA 98114

Dear Jack:

I'm sorry to inform you that I will be leaving on January 26. I want you to know that I've really enjoyed my time here, but feel it's time for me to move on. I appreciate everything you've taught me and will miss everyone in the office.

I hope you can understand my reason for leaving Jack and will accept my resignation. Thank you very much.

Sincerely,

Kevin Michaels

cc: Personnel

Appendix G: Resources

In order to further assist you in achieving a successful job search, I'm providing you with a variety of resources that you may find helpful.

Books

Here is a listing of some books that you may find useful in your quest to gain employment. I've tried to include a nice mix of books on a variety of job-related topics. This way, there's something for everyone. And I tried to keep them pretty current so the information isn't out-of-date.

Adler, Lou, *Hire with Your Head*, John Wiley & Sons, Inc., 2002

Asher, Donald, *The Overnight Resume*, 2nd edition, Ten Speed Press, 1999

Bates, Sunny, *How to Earn What You're Worth*, Mc-Graw Hill, 2004

Beshara, Tony, *The Job Search Solution: The Ultimate System for Finding a Great Job!*, AMACOM, 2006

Betrus, Michael, *Perfect Phrases for Cover Letters*, Mc-Graw Hill, 2006

Betrus, Michael, *Perfect Phrases for Resumes*, Mc-Graw Hill, 2005

Bolles, Richard Nelson, *What Color is Your Parachute 2008*, Ten Speed Press, 2008

DeLuca, Matthew J., and DeLuca, Nanette F., *More Best Answers to the 201 Most Frequently Asked Interview Questions*, Mc-Graw Hill, 2001

Dikel, Margaret Riley, and Roehm, Frances E., *Guide to Internet Job Searching*, 2008-2009 edition, Mc-Graw Hill, 2008

Enelow, Wendy S., and Boldt, Arnold G., *No-Nonsense Cover Letters*, The Career Press, Inc., 2007

Enelow, Wendy S., and Goldman, Shelly, *Insider's Guide to Finding a Job*, JIST Works, 2005

Enelow, Wendy S., *The $100,000+ Job Interview,* Impact Publications, 2005

Enelow, Wendy S., *Best Keywordes for Resumes, Cover Letters, and Interviews,* Impact Publications, 2003

Farr, Michael, and Kursmack, Louise, *15 Minute Cover Letter,* JIST Works, 2005

Farr, Michael, *Next Day Job Interview*, JIST Publishing, 2005

Farr, Michael, *The Quick Resume & Cover Letter Book*, 4th edition, JIST Publishing, 2008

Gale, Linda, *Discover What You're Best At*, Simon and Schuster, 1998

Greene, Brenda, *Get the Interview Every Time*, Dearborn Trade Publishing, 2004

Gregory, Michael, *The Career Chronicles: An Insider's Guide to What Jobs are Really Like*, New World Library, 2008

Hansen, Katherine, and Hansen, Ph.D., Randall, *Dynamic Cover Letters: How to Write the Letter That Gets You the Job,* 3rd edition, Ten Speed Press, 2001

Hawley, Casey, *Job-Winning Answers to the Hardest Interview Questions*, MJF Books, 2001

Kaplan, Robbie Miller, *How to Say It in Your Job Search*, Prentice Hall, 2002

Karsh, Brad, *Confessions of a Recruiting Director: The Insider's Guide to Landing Your First Job*, The Berkley Publishing Group, 2006

Krannich, Ron, and Krannich, Caryl, *I Can't Believe They Asked me That?*, Impact Publications, 2007

Krannich, Ron, and Krannich, Caryl, *Interview for Success: A Practical Guide to Increasing Job Interviews, Offers, and Salaries*, 8th edition, Impact Publications, 2003

Krannich, Ronald L., *Careering and Re-Careering for the 1990's: The Complete Guyide to Planning Your Future*, 2nd edition, Impact Publications, 1991

Krannich, Ph.D., Ron, and Krannich, Ph.D, Caryl, *No One Will Hire Me! Avoid 15 Mistakes and Win the Job*, Impact Publications, 2002

Llewellyn, A. Bronwyn, with Holt, M.A., Robin, *The Everything Career Tests Book*, Adams Media, 2007

Martin, Carole, *Perfect Phrases for the Perfect Interview*, Mc-Graw Hill, 2005

Messmer, Max, *Job Hunting For Dummies*, 2nd edition, IDG Books Worldwide, Inc., 1999

Sachs, Randi Toler, *How to Become a Skillful Interviewer*, AMACOM, 1994

Talyor, Jeff, and Hardy, Doug, *Monster Careers: Interviewing*, Penguine Group, 2005

Wendover, Robert W., *Smart Hiring*, 2nd edition, Sourcebooks, Inc., 1998

Yates, Martin, *Knock 'em Dead 2008*, 21st edition, Adams Media, 2007

Yates, Martin, *Resumes that Knock 'em Dead*, 7th edition, Adams Media, 2006

Yates, Martin, *Cover Letters that Knock 'em Dead*, 7th edition, Adams Media, 2006

Yeager, Neil, and Hough, Lee, *Power Interviews: Job-Winning Tactics from Fortune 500 Recruiters*, John Wiley & Sons, Inc., 1998

Job Interviews That Get You Hired, 1st edition, Learning Express, 2006

Job Hunting Made Easy, Learning Express, LLC, 1997

State Employment Websites

These websites contain information about available jobs, labor market, training programs, and/or unemployment information and filing. Many of them are great places to begin your job search!

Alabama .... Department of Industrial Relations .... dir.alabama.gov
Alaska .... Alaska Job Center Network .... jobs.state.ak.us
Arizona .... Arizona Workforce Connection .... arizonaworkforceconnection.com
Arkansas .... Arkansas Workforce .... arworks.org
California .... CalJOBS .... caljobs.ca.gov
Colorado .... Department of Labor and Employment .... coworkforce.com
Connecticut .... Department of Labor .... ctdol.state.ct.us
Delaware .... Department of Labor .... delawareworks.com
Florida .... Agency for Workforce Innovation .... floridajobs.org
Georgia .... Department of Labor .... dol.state.ga.us
Hawaii .... Department of Human Resources Development .... hawaii.gov/hrd
Idaho .... Department of Commerce & Labor .... cl.idaho.gov
Illinois .... Department of Employment Security .... ides.state.il.us
Indiana .... Department of State Personnel .... in.gov/jobs
Iowa .... Department of Personnel .... state.ia.us/government/idop/index.htm
Kansas .... Department of Labor .... dol.ks.gov/index.htm
Kentucky .... Cabinet for Workforce Development .... workforce.ky.gov
Louisiana .... Department of Labor .... laworks.net
Maine .... Department of Labor .... state.me.us/labor
Maryland .... Department of Labor, Licensing and Regulation .... dllr.state.md.us
Massachusetts .... Division of Employment and Training .... detma.org/default.htm
Michigan .... Department of Career Development .... michigan.gov/mdcd
Minnesota .... Bureau of Mediation Services .... bms.state.mn.us
Mississippi .... Department of Employment Security .... mdes.ms.gov
Missouri .... Department of Labor and Industrial Relations .... dolir.state.mo.us
Montana .... Department of Labor and Industry .... dli.state.mt.us
Nebraska .... Department of Labor .... dol.state.ne.us
Nevada .... Department of Employment, Training and Rehabilitation .... detr.state.nv.us
New Hampshire .... Department of Labor .... labor.state.nh.us
New Jersey .... Department of Labor .... state.nj.us/labor
New Mexico .... Department of Labor .... dol.state.nm.us

New York ....Department of Civil Service .... cs.state.ny.us
North Carolina..........Department of Commerce .... ncesc.com
North Dakota............Department of Labor .... state.nd.us/labor
Ohio ....Bureau of Workers' Compensation .... bwc.state.oh.us
Oklahoma ....Department of Labor .... state.ok.us/~okdol
Oregon.....................Bureau of Labor and Industries .... boli.state.or.us
Pennsylvania.............Department of Labor and Industry ....dli.state.pa.us
Rhode Island ....Department of Labor and Training..dlt.ri.gov
South Carolina..........Employment Security Commission .... sces.org
South Dakota............Bureau of Personnel.. state.sd.us/bop
Tennessee ....Department of Labor & Workforce Development..........................state.tn.us/labor-wfd
Texas ....Texas Rehabilitation Commission .... rehab.state.tx.us
Utah........................Department of Human Resource Management ....dhrm.state.ut.us
Vermont...................Department of Employment and Training...det.state.vt.us
Virginia....................Business and Employment............. virginia.gov/cmsportal/employment_850/index.html
Washington ....WorkSource Washington (Employment Security)....................................... work.wa.gov
West Virginia ....Bureau of Employment Programs.. state.wv.us/bep
Wisconsin ....Department of Workforce Development .... dwd.state.wi.us
Wyoming ....Department of Employment .... wydoe.state.wy.us

Job Boards

These job board websites can help you find and research jobs and professions. And I tried to include something for everyone. Some are general career sites; others are geared towards specific industries or fields. I've also included some that are good for students or those of you considering going back to school.

General

Yahoo! HotJobs .... hotjobs.yahoo.com
Monster .... monster.com
Careerbuilder .... careerbuilder.com
America's Job Bank ....jobbankinfo.org
Indeed ....indeed.com
JobDig ....jobdig.com
JobCentral ....jobcentral.com
Jobs.com ....jobs.com
Jobdango ....jobdango.com
Craigslist .... craigslist.org

Salary Information

Salary information and job search .... salary.com
Salary information .... salaryexpert.com

Career Guidance and Job Market Information

Career Guide to Industries .... bls.gov/oco/cg
America's Career Info Net... careerinfonet.org
Occupational Outlook Quarterly .... bls.gov/opub/ooq/ooqhome.htm
Occupational Outlook Handbook.. bls.gov/oco
Employment projections .... bls.gov/emp
State Occupational Projections .... projectionscentral.com
Career Advantage .... careeradvantage.org
Career One Stop...careeronestop.org
Career Journal .... careerjournal.com
Job Hunter's Bible ....jobhuntersbible.com

Education and Training Providers and Information

College Navigator..nces.ed.gov/collegenavigator
Peterson's College Guide and Ratings ....petersons.com
Financial Aid Information and Sources...finaid.org

Student and Part-Time Employment

Temporary.. net-temps.com
Students .... studentjobs.com
Internships ....internshipprograms.com
Seasonal Work .... backdoorjobs.com
Seasonal Work .... coolworks.com
Summer.. summerjobs.com
Volunteering Opportunities... volunteermatch.org
Peace Corps .... peacecorps.com

Industry and Career Specific

Academic (faculty, staff, administration) ....chronicle.com
Automotive (technical and service) ....autojobs.com
Computer and High-Tech ....dice.com
Engineering.. engcen.com
Federal Government...fedworld.gov/jobs/jobsearch.html
Financial Services .... jobsinthemoney.com
Healthcare.. medzilla.com
Media (television and radio) .... tvandradiojobs.com
Non-Profit.......................content.opportunityknocks.org/info~non-profit-job-search.php
Scientific .... sciencecareers.sciencemag.org
Telecommuting (working from home).. telecomcareers.net

Notes

Notes

Notes

www.ingramcontent.com/pod-product-compliance
Lightning Source LLC
Chambersburg PA
CBHW080010210526
45170CB00015B/1966